SING OVER ME

Dennis Jernigan

Published by
Innovo Publishing LLC
www.innovopublishing.com
1-888-546-2111

Providing Full-Service Publishing Services for
Christian Authors, Artists & Organizations: Hardbacks, Paperbacks,
eBooks, Audiobooks, Music & Film

SING OVER ME

Scripture quotations taken from the New American Standard Bible®,
Copyright © 1960, 1962, 1963, 1968, 1971, 1972, 1973, 1975, 1977, 1995
by The Lockman Foundation. Used by permission.

Library of Congress Control Number: 2014902108
ISBN 13: 978-1-61314-176-2

Cover Design & Interior Layout: Innovo Publishing LLC

Printed in the United States of America
U.S. Printing History

First Edition: February 2014

ACKNOWLEDGMENTS

Without my wife, Melinda, I could never have come to the place of healing and deliverance and joy I now walk in.

Without my children who have taught me so much about God's love for me, I would not be able to comprehend the level of God's love for me I now enjoy.

Without my parents and brothers and extended family, I would never have come to the place of grace and safety in which I feel safe enough to even share my story.

Without my grandchildren and those yet to be born in the Jernigan lineage, I would not have seen the beauty and strength of legacy nor would I have found the courage to share.

Without the myriad of people who have had a hand in my healing (and are far too numerous to name here), I would never have survived.

Without the trials, without the fire, without the wounds upon wounds, without the persecution I now experience, and without the naysayers, I could not have been refined.

Without my friends, Danny and Joanna, I would feel less cared for in this world.

Without the mentoring of heroes like Jack Taylor and Annie Herring and Keith Green, I would not have experienced the Kingdom perspective so fully.

Without the brave people at Innovo, I would not feel so un-alone.

Without the massive number of people who have told me through the years that the hearing of my story set them on a path of freedom in telling their own stories, I would not feel so needed.

Without the presence of my Father, the work of Jesus the Son, and the power of the Holy Spirit, I would be nothing.

Thank you,
Dennis Jernigan

TABLE OF CONTENTS

PROLOGUE

More than thirty years ago, I left behind a homosexual way of thinking about myself. For twenty-two years, I thought a homosexual was who I was—who I was created or destined to be. But it was simply humanism—man-centered theology—that led me to that belief. It was through an encounter with Jesus Christ that I was given a brand-new identity. What I discovered along this incredible journey of freedom from same-sex attraction is that God's best and man's best are not one and the same. In fact, God's been setting men free from same-sex attraction for thousands of years. Homosexuality is no bigger deal to God than any other addiction or upside-down way of thinking. Here's how I know that. This text from the Apostle Paul to the church in Corinth was written almost two thousand years ago:

> Or do you not know that the unrighteous will not inherit the kingdom of God? Do not be deceived; neither fornicators, nor idolaters, nor adulterers, nor *effeminate*, nor *homosexuals*, nor thieves, nor the covetous, nor drunkards, nor revilers, nor swindlers, will inherit the kingdom of God. Such **were** some of you; but you were washed, but you were sanctified, but you were justified in the name of the Lord Jesus Christ and in the Spirit of our God (1 Corinthians 6:9–11 NASB).

Telling my story is not easy, even though I've shared thousands of times over the past twenty-four years. Why so difficult now? Two main reasons.

Society's—our culture's—way of thinking about all things homosexual has shifted dramatically. It seems that most people either don't want to be seen as a bigot, or they actually have come to believe that same-sex attraction is normal. From personal experience I know this to be far from the truth. Nevertheless, it seems at times as if I'm the only one telling a different story—like I'm swimming upstream against the flow. I know this is not true because I've met thousands of others who walk in freedom from same-sex attraction, but the feeling IS true.

The other reason this is so difficult is that I have to walk the tightrope of how much to share. I'll do my best to spare you the nitty-gritty details of my sexual encounters, but more importantly, I'll do my best to protect the identities of those who would rather I not divulge information about them. In order to spare them or their families any undue embarrassment, I've chosen to give pseudonyms to those individuals and have altered the location of certain events.

What follows is MY story. My past does not define me. My present circumstances do not define me. The things that tempt me do not define me. The gay community does not define me. No man has that honor or power. My identity comes from my Maker and from Him alone. But what a journey it has been to get me to that place of truth and understanding!

Why call the book Sing Over Me? Because many years ago, God began to get my attention through music, even when I didn't know it was Him. And then I discovered a couple of things about God and HIS music:

You are my hiding place; You preserve me from trouble; You surround me with songs of deliverance (Psalm 32:7 NASB).

He says He surrounds me with songs of deliverance! As I look back on my life in the writing of this book, it is easy to "hear" how He was actually there each and every step of the way. But wait . . . there's more!

> The LORD your God in your midst, The Mighty
> One, will save; He will rejoice over you with gladness,
> He will quiet you with His love, He will rejoice over
> you with singing (Zephaniah 3:17 NKJV).

God rejoices over ME! In song! No matter what! He just loves me. Loved me all along. Has actually ALWAYS been there singing HIS songs of love and rejoicing over me, gracefully weaving His sweet melodies of grace and mercy and redemption and restoration so magnificently and creatively in and through my life, even when I turned my back on Him. Why call the book *Sing Over Me*? Because that's exactly what He does. He sings over me.

As you read this, it is my honest prayer that Jesus Christ would bring you to a greater awareness of Who He is and what that could mean for your life. And that you too would learn to hear Him singing His songs of deliverance, love, and rejoicing . . . over YOU!

Dennis Jernigan

WHEN EVERYTHING CHANGED

I remember many things about my childhood. Happy things. Happy times. Like fishing with my dad and mom. Sitting on the pond bank intently watching for even the slightest movement of my bobber. Hoping mine would be the next to disappear beneath the muddy water so I could pull back on the line and feel the rush of adrenaline as the fish took my bait and pulled the bobber completely out of sight.

Happy times. Riding horses with my dad and brothers.

Happy times. Playing spotlight in the dark for hours on end with my siblings and cousins.

Happy times. Watching my dad grind the grain and make flour. Milking the cows every morning. Helping my mom pull potato bugs off the leaves of the tender plants in our garden. Having contests with my little brothers to see who could pee the furthest from the window in the loft of the barn. Chasing down grasshoppers for bait. The many fishing contests between me and my brothers and cousins— hundreds of little perch. Swimming in Shale Pit as my parents had done when they were my age, a rite of passage.

Happy times. My mom taking out a small loan from the bank just so me and my brothers could have some new toys. My dad working two or three jobs at a time just to meet our needs. As I look back now, it becomes painfully obvious that we really didn't have much. But how precious to realize that we boys never knew the feeling of that reality at all! From my perspective, we had everything we could possibly need. We were truly happy.

As I reflect on my life, I realize there was far more good than bad. Remembering certain things from my childhood transports me back to a happy time in my life and fills me with an abiding sense of wonder and joy. But that wonder and joy are also mixed with a certain melancholy I can't deny or get away from. Amidst the happy times, darkness came into my life and added a tinge of ongoing sorrow to the mix.

My aunt and uncle owned a stockyard in Okmulgee, Oklahoma. Every Saturday was a sale day. Every other Monday was horse sale day. And I LOVED going to the sale barn with my mom. She and her sisters, along with my grandpa Herman and grandma Lela, helped out each week. Mom and her sisters worked in the office while Grandma worked in the kitchen, leaving Grandpa to help with the tack sale and the herding of livestock.

There was always a bit of excitement. Like the time us kids were playing outside at my cousin's house that sat on the sale barn property and our moms came running, screaming, "Get in the house! Get in the house NOW!" Only after we ran inside and our parents joined us did we learn that a wild Brahma bull had escaped and was running amok in our vicinity!

Like the time my aunt Patsy was laughing at a joke and slapped her hand down on the office counter right onto the very sharp and pointed receipt spike that instantly pierced THROUGH her hand!

Like the time the Frisco train engineered by my uncle Ivan ran into a pickup truck that tried to beat the train across the track that ran directly in front of the stockyard entrance . . . and didn't make it in time. Regardless of what happened at the sale barn, there was always a sense of adventure and excitement when Saturday approached. I dearly loved my times spent there.

What joy it was to watch as the many trucks pulling livestock trailers took turns backing up to the loading chutes. My brothers, cousins, and I could hardly stand the wait, wondering what amazing creature would appear next. Of course, cattle of all shapes and sizes was the norm—Angus, Hereford, Charlais, Guernsey, Holstein. And most exciting of all was when a Brahma would come through!

We were intrigued by this humpbacked, exotic breed from India. Most commonly used for bucking contests at rodeos, their perceived wildness was not lost on us kids. And when one began to appear from the recesses of a cattle trailer or cattle truck, we always got goose bumps and prepared to jump down from our perches along the stockyard fence just in case it lunged for us! How dangerous it seemed to us!

Almost as equally exciting to see emerge from a backed-up trailer were any number of animals. Coming in all shapes and sizes, pigs were always fun to watch. We would giggle away at all the oinking and squealing and would almost fall off the fence with laughter whenever one of the babies would squeak and squall when separated, even for a second, from her massive mother.

Sheep and goats were always so exotic in my mind, as were donkeys and mules. I don't necessarily know WHY I deemed them exotic; they just were. But the most exotic of all was the day a BISON came through. What a strange and wondrous feeling to see something that, up until that day, I had only seen in John Wayne movies! And imagine my ecstasy and joy the day my dad brought home a bison calf for us to bottle-feed! I LOVED the sale barn and the many adventures I experienced there. But little did I know how one particular experience would change everything.

It was a spring Saturday like so many others I had experienced at that little stockyard. Spending much of our time watching the unloading of animals, my brothers and cousins had decided to explore the stock pens. Like expert tightrope walkers, we traversed the entire stockyard, which seemed so massive to us. Starting in the cattle area, we edged our way to the swine holding pens, and from there made our way to the sheep and goats, and then all the way back to where we had started, laughing and daring one another to even greater feats of bravery every step of the way. Who will touch the Brahma's hump? Who will make the piglet squeal? Who can ride a sheep? Who can catch a goat?

After a morning of adventure, I found myself needing to pee very badly. With so many people around and no trees to pee behind, I knew the men's room on the south side of the main barn was nearby, so I told the boys to wait on me so I could run to pee. Making it into the room just before it was too late, I relieved myself in the first open stool I could find.

I hadn't noticed the man before, but as I turned around, he was there. I saw his feet first but then noticed that his pants were down— his underwear, too. The only grown man I had seen naked up until that point had been my daddy. What I saw made me feel very uncomfortable. The man pointed at his penis and said, "Touch it." I ran.

Running as fast as I could from the small men's room, I ran toward the door to the sale barn office where I knew I could find my mom. As I ran, a very curious thought began to take place in my mind. If I could forget it, I would, but I can't forget it. The thought at first seemed innocuous enough. *Why did that man do that?* I could not figure out why he would try to do that to ME. And then that thought led to, *Why did that man think that I would want to touch him there?*

From that point, my mind began to feel like a ping-pong table, thoughts bouncing every which way. *Why did he ask me to do that? Did he think I would want to touch him there? He must have. Why else would he ask? Something must be wrong with me!*

And you know what I did next? I stopped running. Why? Because I began to think of myself in a very different way than I had thought up until that point. My conclusion? Something must be wrong with me. Why else would that man think he could ask me to do that unless something was wrong with me?

As I look back, I realize now that I had become very self-focused on that moment. Regardless of whether I was victimized or not, I began to be fully focused on myself and making sure no one else could see just how flawed I was. One moment I was a carefree, adventurous, and normal little boy. In the next moment everything changed—forever.

PERCEPTIONS

After the incident in the men's room, I began to think of myself as being "different" than other little boys. This belief soon became reinforced in several various ways. Being very artistic and very emotionally sensitive, it didn't take very long to be labeled a sissy—even in first grade!

Mrs. Ross, my first-grade teacher, was a great instructor. Being a musician herself, she was very encouraging when she learned I could play the piano. She loved art of all kinds and admonished us to express ourselves in an artistic manner during our daily art class. At first, art class was for learning the basics—how to draw shapes and to color inside the lines, but then we progressed to drawing simple shapes like houses and barns, and soon trees and flowers and landscapes, and then to experimenting with drawing animals. But my favorite thing to draw, at least in first grade, was people.

Still emblazoned upon my mind was the glowing review Mrs. Ross gave of my picture of an Indian maiden, complete with braids and a feather. Placing my picture in the most prominent place above the chalkboard—a place each and every student knew to be the most treasured, most coveted, most longed-for position—she described to the entire class what was so extraordinary about my drawing.

How proud I was as she described the proper use of proportion and depth. How special I felt as she encouraged the other students to use my drawing as an example of all the right ways to use color, perspective, and depth perception. Even some of my fellow students seemed to ooh and aah in amazement as Mrs. Ross went on and on about my artistic prowess. Mostly the girls.

My bubble would burst soon enough, though, and it didn't take long. During the morning recess, we all ran to our favorite piece of playground equipment. Some ran straight for the swings. Others ran frantically to the merry-go-round, while still others ran to the see-saw. Me? I ran straight for the monkey bars!

Trying to be the first to the top, the place of lordship over the playground, I hurriedly climbed. Several other boys were vying for the same piece of playground real estate, each bound and determined to be crowned king. Just as I neared the top of the monkey bars, and just as I reached to pull myself into position, an older boy, Lonnie, pushed me away, almost causing me to tumble all the way down. Had I not clung to the bar, I would have crashed to the ground. Hanging there in hurt and disbelief, my ego took an unexpected and very direct hit as Lonnie chided me.

"Get out of here, sissy-boy! Go color with the girls where you belong!" Taken aback at how quickly news had traveled concerning my artistic triumph, my now-bruised ego was further crushed when one of my first-grade classmates joined in the verbal barrage.

"Yeah, sissy-boy!" teased Reggie, obviously trying to impress the older boy. Turning to Lonnie, he said, "I told you he was like a girl!"

"Get off the monkey bars before you hurt yourself, sissy-boy!" yelled Lonnie. "Go play with the girls where you belong!"

Still hanging by one hand, hanging on for dear life, I finally managed to get down from the precarious position I had suddenly found myself in, and at the same time managed to hold back the tears threatening to expose my utter humiliation. Walking away in defeat, I turned to find several other boys pointing at me and whispering. Embarrassed and confused, I sulked away in horror pretending I was all right on the outside while devastated on the inside.

Meanwhile, many of the girls had seen what had happened and immediately ran to me and began consoling me. They then turned their attention to Lonnie and began to scold him on my behalf, which only emboldened the boy to continue his barrage from high atop his throne on the monkey bars for the entire grade-school student body to hear.

"Look at the sissy-boy, everyone! He has to have girls take up for him! What a fag!" yelled Lonnie at the top of his lungs. "Somebody needs to give him a hug before he starts cryin'!"

Turning back toward the yelling boy, I cried out in defiance the worst thing I could think of to call him. "Shut up, sh**-head!" And then all hell broke loose!

Jumping down from his perch, the now-seething Lonnie ran at me, pushing me in the chest, causing me to fall backwards onto my rear end. "Who you callin' sh**-head, faggot?" Being younger than Lonnie, I was no physical match for the bigger boy, but I got up anyway—or at least I tried. Before I could fully get to my feet, Lonnie was on top of me, forcing me back to the ground, pummeling me with his fists.

"If you know what's good for you, you'll stay down, boy!" screamed the raging boy.

By now I was so full of fury all I could think of was hitting the boy with every ounce of strength I could muster, but I found myself unable to do a thing to defend myself because he had both of my arms pinned to the ground. Now humiliated by the laughter of my peers—not one of the boys I called friend daring to help me in any way, shape, or form—I could no longer hold back my tears. As I began to sob, the boy spat in my face and then let me up as he slapped me one last time.

I simply sat there crying while the boys all walked away laughing. Only my friend, Cliff, came to help me up. Cliff was an African American boy. As he helped me up, Lonnie turned around and said, "Help him up, nigger, and I'll kick your ass, too! Leave the sissy-boy to get up on his own. Let's see if he can even do that."

Cliff helped me up anyway, and Lonnie just shook his head and walked away with his chest stuck out, bragging of his greatness to his newfound entourage.

That day I learned many valuable lessons that would serve me well in the years to come. Lonnie, as he grew older, seemed to live to make my life miserable and to remind me of how worthless a human being I was for being so different.

I heard the word *fag* for the first time and would be puzzled by what it could possibly mean for several more years.

I learned that being different was not such a good thing in the eyes of many.

I learned that the color of one's skin was a big deal to some people as well.

I learned that if I was to survive emotionally, I would have to portray myself as something I thought people wanted. Whatever that "something" was, I was intent on finding it because if I couldn't, my life would prove to be miserable.

That day, coupled with my stockyard men's room experience, I determined my self-perception was somehow wrong—that being me was somehow wrong—and that would have to change.

REAL LITTLE BOY
IN A MAN'S WORLD

My next sexual encounter came in a very innocent way. While spending the night with a friend during my first-grade year of school, we stripped down to our underwear as little boys do when it's bedtime. Noticing he looked very similar to me, I began to wonder if EVERYTHING of his compared to mine. As we lay in bed, our conversation covered all manner of topics. When he asked me if I had a penis, I became very excited because I was wondering the same thing about him! I simply said yes. He immediately responded with, "Me, too! Want to feel it?" Before I could respond, he went on to say, "I'll let you feel mine if you let me feel yours." I naively agreed.

Our mutual fondling lasted all of ten seconds. Having our mutual curiosity satisfied, we went on to the next subject and never mentioned that moment again in all the years I've known him. Though I hadn't realized it at the time, something had been awakened in me that night that I would have a most difficult time keeping in check for a major portion of my life.

So many episodes and events went into shaping my mind as a boy. To say I was confused would be a vast understatement. One of the most telling examples is the fact that I would never put my hands in my pockets as boys do. I've even tried to find photographic evidence to the contrary, but those photos do not exist. It was not until I began to walk in freedom from same-sex attraction in my early twenties that I felt confident enough in my masculine identity to walk around or stand around with other guys with my hands in my pockets. Why did I not put my hands in my pockets? Because that's what real boys do, and I was not a real boy. I was something different. Something less.

Growing up in rural Oklahoma it did not take a rocket scientist to figure out that this was the realm of he-men. Manly men. Man's men. And my dad was seen as a man's man. I was so proud of him. My dad could rope a calf. My dad could take apart a broken engine and put it back together and make it run like a top. My dad could saddle a horse. My dad could weld metal together and create amazing works of art, like the old wagon wheels he converted into an entrance gate to our farm, complete with hand-forged letters spelling out the name Jernigan across the top. My dad could play basketball. My dad could play the guitar. My dad could sing. My dad was a basketball referee. My dad could do ANYTHING!

When I was about four years old, my dad and mom bought the local Sinclair station. I loved going to the station for many reasons. The mascot, the logo, was a brontosaur. What boy doesn't love a brontosaur? How cool it was in my little boy mind to imagine that we owned the only dinosaur in town? Those were the days before self-serve gasoline. This was a real filling station—a service station.

How proud I was of my dad. I remember watching him run out to each car or pickup as it drove into the service area. As the customer rolled down his window (we used to say "cranked" down his window in the days before power windows), he would greet my dad with "Fill 'er up!" And then my dad would ask if they wanted regular or ethyl. For the longest time I couldn't understand why my dad seemed to offer them some lady named Ethel! (Little boy memories.)

Once the type of fuel was established and the nozzle inserted into the fuel receptacle, my dad would ask them to "pop the hood".

Like clockwork, he proceeded to check the oil and other vital automotive fluids. Once that task was completed, he went to washing the windows, carefully getting each and every spot, making the windows shine. It was so amazing to see how far my dad could reach, not leaving one bug smatter on even the furthest reaches of the windshield. I don't know if my dad ever noticed, but I would often mimic the very actions he would go through while servicing a customer's car. I wanted to be just like him.

During down times, whenever there were lulls in business, my dad would let me put on my roller skates and tool around the pavement surrounding the station. Since we lived on a farm, there was no place to roller skate, so we kept my skates at the station in town. One day as I skated around and around the gasoline pumps, a small group of men—good ol' boys, my daddy used to call them—sat around in the shade talking and chewing tobacco. After a few minutes, I decided to do a very manly thing. I skated up to my dad (who never chewed tobacco or smoked a cigarette or drank one drop of alcohol) and boldly asked if I could try some chewing tobacco.

He grinned sheepishly and winked at the other men and quickly said, "Sure." The men all began to encourage me and seemed almost overjoyed that I would dare to do such a manly thing. One of the men took a packet from his pocket and opened it. Immediately the air was filled with the sweetest, most heavenly smelling concoction I had ever smelled until that point in my life. In fact, it is a smell that lives on in my memory to this day.

Taking what seemed to be a much-too-big-for-a-little-boy's-mouth portion, he told me to put the chaw in my cheek and just hold it there. Full of pride and wonder, I did what I had seen the men do so many times before. I put the big fat chaw in my mouth and promptly and proudly went back to skating. As I scooted off I noticed the men eyeing me. My assumption was that they were excited for me and proud of me for crossing this threshold of manhood. Boy, was I wrong!

Like a ticking time bomb, the men were holding their collective breath waiting for it to happen. And happen it did. Before I knew it, I began to grow dizzy. Now light-headed and woozy, I began to stumble around on my skates. Not wanting to be seen as weak, I defiantly kept the chaw in my mouth and tried to continue skating. It was not long until I skated straight into my dad's arms, retching my guts out. Through tears of embarrassment, I told my dad, "I never want to do that again!" His words to me? "I hope you learned your lesson!"

While I still recall that particular event in detail, the embarrassment never crossed the line to humiliation. It was truly a good lesson for me, teaching me that just because others enjoy a certain activity doesn't mean I will—or that it's good for me! Still, a part of me would continue to associate chewing tobacco with being a real man for quite some time.

For years my dad ran the farm and worked full time at a mechanic garage doing car repair and tractor maintenance for farmers for miles in every direction. He would wake me every morning to milk the two cows before I went to school, and then he would be off to hay the small herd of cattle we kept. In the winter time we would go break the ice on the ponds to make a place for the cows to drink. In the springtime we would round up all the cattle and vaccinate the newborn calves and castrate the newborn males. Every few weeks during the summer, my brothers and I would round up the cows and put them in the corral so my dad could spray them for flies and other parasites. I honestly don't understand how my dad got everything done.

His reputation was one of hard work and goodness. When men would come into the garage to order a part or to inquire as to getting their vehicle repaired, I would listen while they spoke amongst one another. More often than not, I heard phrases like "That Robert Jernigan is a good man" or "He does a good job for a fair price." And how many times did my dad get a call to come to some stranded driver's aid or a call to come and help a farmer get his tractor going so the field could be tilled? Countless. My dad's reputation made me proud to be a Jernigan.

As a young boy, I truly needed my dad's affirmation and approval. Because I thought of myself as something less than a real boy, I felt great pressure to measure up to my dad's standards of work and his standards of doing things well. In MY mind, I never measured up. That wasn't my dad's fault. That was my PERCEPTION—my personal interpretation of what would please my father.

Being a creative kid with a flair for the artistic and dramatic, I was prone to mountainous emotional highs and the deepest of emotional lows. Not only was this confusing to me, but I'm convinced it was confusing for my dad as well. There were many times when he'd give me a job to do, like sweeping the entire repair shop floor, which was massive. Upon his inspection, he might point out a few spots I had missed and I'd feel worthless, like I didn't measure up. There were times when he'd tell me to clean the tools and put them back in their proper place, and I never quite seemed to get them clean enough or put them in exactly the right spot. At least that was MY perception. My dad loved me; I just couldn't see how.

There were a few times when my dad became so frustrated with my moodiness or sullen behavior that he erupted in anger. Not only did I not understand my own feelings, but I most certainly had no frame of reference for communicating my feelings in the slightest, which was frustrating to EVERYONE! On one occasion, I had willfully not done one of my chores, preferring to delay it until the last possible moment so I could play just a few minutes longer. In exasperation, my dad whipped off his belt and began to tan my butt—which I deserved—but on this day, I had driven him off the edge and right into taking his frustration out on me.

So loud were my cries and so fierce was his anger that my mom and my grandmother Jernigan intervened, begging my dad to stop. And he did. I deserved the punishment. I had so disappointed my dad that he felt he had no other recourse but to beat the insolence out of me. Did my dad react too harshly? No doubt. Was he sorry? Of course. Did he ever do it again? No. Was I changed? You bet. How? I knew I had been disobedient, and at the same time I became aware that there was no way I could ever please my dad if I could not be obedient to him. Although I may not have known what to call it, I began to base my worth on how well I performed for my dad and others. And in my twelve-year-old mind on the day of that beating, the next logical step was this: if my dad ever found out what I was really like—that I was like a girl—I would be rejected. The difference between him finding out what I was truly like on the inside and me keeping it hidden was easily boiled down to one word: performance.

It was not any great stretch of the imagination for me to realize this was my "truth" than the day I performed well on the Little League baseball team my dad coached. When I got that first hit, my dad became so excited and began showering praise on me! Not only my dad, but ALL the other guys! Perform well, I am affirmed. Perform well, I am accepted. Perform well, I am loved. Even though I did not feel like a real little boy, I could at least perform like one. Still I could never, ever bring myself to put my hands in my pockets. It seemed so unnatural. After all, I wasn't a real little boy. And my dad—a great man I could never measure up to in my mind—would never find out if I could help it.

A CLUELESS BOY

I hesitate in writing this chapter because I'm not sure exactly where the line is between sharing enough to get the point across or in not sharing enough—so I'll just dive right in!

Growing up on a farm, I had more than enough opportunities to see nature run its course in full sexual exposure. Living down the road from a horse ranch, I saw a stallion mounting a mare on more than one occasion. Having raised cattle since my earliest memories, I've seen more than my fair share of bulls mounting cows. In my days before puberty hit, I had absolutely no idea what was going on. I didn't understand or feel the need to question why the male animals seemed to occasionally thrust their penises into seemingly VERY patient females!

When you're ten years old and clueless as to the purpose of sex, sexual activity among animals is at best innocuous and at worst a bit embarrassing. I'll never forget the day I was helping my dad herd the cattle into a small corral in order to bunch them close enough to make spraying for pests more efficient, wasting less time, effort, and water in the process. Noticing the bull paying extra-special attention to a nearby female, I knew something was about to happen. Suddenly, the bull extended his male member, mounted the cow, and missed the insertion, sending a twenty-foot-long stream of semen flying above the pair and dousing several other cows in proximity! I turned to my dad to see his reaction, and he didn't even seem to notice. So I paid it little attention. But I couldn't stop thinking about what I had just seen.

My first sexual experience, even though I had run from the scene, had been the man exposing himself to me in the sale barn men's room. Since that moment, I had taken great interest in my own anatomy, wondering if I would one day look like my dad—like that guy. Because I had a very warped view of my own masculinity, I had taken a turn toward the perverse. Now before you get your panties in a wad, as we say here in the south, here is my definition of perversion: taking something God intended for a holy purpose and using it in a way He never intended. Sex was intended for a holy purpose. Sex was intended for the marriage bed between a man and a woman. Sex was intended for procreation first. Sex was intended for comfort, pleasure, and intimacy. I had no clue about all of that. We NEVER talked about sexual matters in church. Ever.

It had never dawned on me that one day my body would begin to change from that of a boy into that of a man. Since my dad and mom had never talked with me about anything concerning what puberty would mean and never even remotely mentioned anything of the sexual nature, I was woefully left to traverse the minefield of puberty all by myself.

It seemed as though puberty hit me with all its force when I was eleven years old. Hair began to sprout under my arms and in my pubic area. At first, I thought something was wrong with me, so I tried to shave the hair away. Having no resources with which to purchase razors, and much too embarrassed to ask my dad or mom for them, imagine my delight the day I discovered my grandpa Herman's stash!

Grandpa Herman, my mom's dad, was constantly buying large quantities of various toiletries, like hair creme, hand lotion, soap, shaving creme, and razors. He was what was referred to as a "jobber," someone who purchases items at wholesale cost and then resells them. He was constantly buying odd lots of every imaginable thing that might bring a pretty penny. One day he showed me his latest lot of goods and proceeded to tell me I could have anything I needed. This was such wonderful news! I could get the tools necessary to rid myself of that pesky underarm hair without the embarrassment of asking for any of it!

Stealing away into a private place, I proceeded to lather up my underarms and pubic area and put razor to flesh, only to cut myself so often that I wanted to give up in frustration. But I completed the task and stood back in front of the mirror as little droplets of blood streamed down my side from under my armpits and still more streamed down my thighs. And then the stinging began to set in. How would I ever keep up with this if it hurt so badly? What was I to do? The mere thought of someone else possibly noticing my changing appearance brought such deep fear to my soul that I was bound and determined to keep anyone from seeing it. I would just get through this current physical pain and simply cover myself to keep others from noticing.

During that summer, I kept my shirt on out of sheer fear of being found out to have hair growing out of the weirdest places on my body. Looking back, I now realize this was simply one more scheme of the enemy to keep me as self-focused as possible. Being a farm boy and having lots of brothers and male cousins, it was very noticeable during our swim sessions and normal play to be the only boy with a shirt on. To take my shirt off was the most dreadful thing I could think of. But that all was compounded when one day my aunt said to me, "What's that growing there on your upper lip?"

As soon as I realized what she meant by that, I ran away mortified at this "embarrassment" and right into the bathroom, locking the door behind me as quickly as I could. Sure enough, there were tiny dark hairs sprouting on my upper lip! My thoughts? *How could I get rid of this without anyone noticing and without bringing any more undue attention to myself?* My dream was that somehow all this change would simply stop, and I could be left alone. But nature has a way of happening whether we are ready for it or not.

No one ever took me aside and explained that I would need deodorant. It was one of my cousins who pointed out to me how foul my body smelled. Taking a whiff of my underarms, I discovered, much to my horror, that she was right! Soon enough, my granddad Herman came through once again. It seemed that always, at just the right moment, he would show me his latest variety of wares, and there, calling out to me like a beacon in the night, was a bottle of Ban roll-on deodorant!

All of these changes taking place in my physical body took a heavy toll on my mental state. My fear was that everyone was judging me. My fear was that somehow someone would tease me or ridicule me because of my appearance. My fear was that everyone would notice how immature I seemed when compared to other boys my age. From my eleven-year-old perspective, it seemed every other boy easily made the transformation from boy to man physically. One boy in my class that fall already had chest hair and a full beard! And he sounded like a man as well!

And wouldn't you know it? My voice—my own voice—began to betray me. It was as if everything I had experienced up to that point was somehow less noticeable. But now every time I opened my mouth, it sounded as if a flock of geese was speaking through me! Like some evil ventriloquist taking control of my body, try as I might I could not keep myself from squawking! Mortified—that was my constant state of being. Couple the great need I felt to be seen as good based on my performance with this new desire to never be seen or heard, and you have the formula for one confused and clueless pre-teen boy!

But none of that compares with the sheer and utter confusion of the strangest trick of all my body began to play on me. It happened the first time during an altar call at church. I was sitting there minding my own business when all of a sudden, the pastor asked everyone to stand and open their hymnals for the invitational hymn. As I stood, I found standing most uncomfortable. Why? I looked down, and much to my horror, my penis had chosen that time to stand to attention! A spontaneous erection! Sitting back down so as to hide this pup tent my pants had become, my mother took notice and told me in a very stern whisper to, "Stand up right now, young man!"

What was I to do? Taking the nearest hymnal and placing it strategically in front of my groin area, I stood up as carefully and swiftly as I could without drawing too much attention to that which I was trying to hide. Now, not only would I have to contend with the hair and odors my body was spontaneously producing, but I had to contend with the constant and very real possibility of the much-dreaded spontaneous erection.

Puberty was Hell on earth for me. Already reeling from the awareness that I was not like other boys, I felt as if I was the only one who had ever had to go through something as horrific as what I was now going through. I know, as I look back, that this was the furthest thing from the truth, but the enemy used my self-awareness and self-focus to keep me from seeing anyone or any hope or any help, even if it was staring me in the face.

And as the enemy would have it, he was only beginning to carry out his extensive plan for my life—for my demise, my plunge—into the world of homosexual thought.

THE SEX TALK
AND OTHER MYTHS

By the time I was ten years old and a year before puberty set in, I was confronted with a harsh reality concerning what other men thought of homosexuals. At this age, I had no clue as to what to call my attraction to other males until the day I overheard the men of my church talking.

One Sunday morning after Sunday School, I found myself playing on the church steps with my brothers and my cousins, as we did almost every Sunday. As we played, the men stood nearby and talked. These were the men I respected most in my life. These were the men who taught me everything I knew about God. These men were like God to me. When their conversation began to be filled with words I had already heard—fags and queers—I found that the word homosexual seemed to mean the same thing to them.

This was the first time I remember thinking that this must be what I was, and then I felt the heat of the realization of what that meant to these men go all over my entire being. I kept playing with my brothers and cousins, but I kept a very deft ear to this conversation. It suddenly dawned on me that if this is what God's men think of me, then that must be what God thinks of me. They hate homosexuals. God must hate homosexuals. God hates me.

I found myself feeling utter hopelessness, and I was only ten years old. I concluded at that time that if I could help it, no one would ever find out my secret. As I look back, is it any wonder I began to perform my way through life for the acceptance and affirmation—and love—that I needed most?

With all of the chaos the onset of puberty was bringing into my life, I could not stop thinking about sexual things. At the same time, I knew that I was so different from other boys I had to maintain a positive outward facade to keep everyone from seeing what I was truly like on the inside.

Soon after the trauma of that first in-church spontaneous erection, I discovered self-fulfillment—masturbation. No need to go into detail here. After this discovery, I found that much comfort from my many fears could be realized by this one, brief act. Even though the relief was temporary, I did experience moments of utter release and moments in which the cares of the world seemed very distant. After a few brief seconds of revelry, my thoughts always gave way to guilt and shame at what I had just done. The guilt and shame and need to perform seemed to lead to yet more episodes of self-stimulation and to yet more guilt and shame and pressure to perform. Without knowing it, I had fallen into a vicious cycle I saw no way of ever escaping from.

As I look back, it's no wonder my feelings of being different from other boys became very sexualized. What should have been a mystery for me—the female persona—is what I actually identified with. My artistic sensibilities and emotional sensitivities were my primary means of expression. Because of my misunderstanding of all things masculine, men became the mystery for me—in every way.

Because I was constantly teased for my effeminate ways, this "truth" was daily reinforced in my psyche. I didn't think like a man, so what must a man's thoughts be like? I didn't feel like a man, so what must a real man's emotions be like? I didn't carry myself like other boys, so what must a real man do to be seen as manly? I didn't understand my own male body, so what was another man's body like? Couple all those confusing thoughts with my male curiosity, and you have the makings of lustful cravings to discover the realities of another man's body.

All of these things I encountered, I encountered long before the reality of the Internet. In those days, boys tended to get their information from other boys, and since the information I received from other boys constantly reminded me how much of a fag and queer I was—how different I was from other boys—I felt as if I was floundering around, much like a ping-pong ball being batted around a room of solid concrete. What joy and self-discovery I found—what a grand resource for me—the day my mom bought that set of *The Encyclopedia Brittanica*! As I pored over the books, it didn't take long for me to get to the "S" volume and go directly to the heading, "sex".

I discovered what the meaning of sexual intercourse was. I saw pictures of the male body and the female body. I briefly glanced over the female image since I had no attraction to it whatsoever yet felt drawn like a magnet to the scientific artistic rendering of the male body, often spending hours mesmerized in wonder at the image before me. These "study sessions" always ended with masturbation and the all-too-familiar cycle of guilt and shame. This constantly recurring cycle eventually brought me to the point of desperation. I would talk with my dad about all of this.

It took me several days to finally get up the nerve to talk with my dad. Having no frame of reference for even how to approach him, I simply said to him one night as he was preparing for bed, "Dad, can I talk to you about something?"

"Sure," he said. "What is it?"

I could feel my face turning red and my hands beginning to shake and my knees to wobble. "Could we talk somewhere privately? Can we go into the bathroom?"

Living in a small house, there were not many private places, and the bathroom was the only room with a lock on the door, so we walked in, and dad closed the door behind us.

"What is it?" my dad asked.

Hem-hawing around, it dawned on me that I didn't even know what I wanted or needed to ask, so I just sheepishly began with, "Sometimes when I wake up in the morning, there's white, sticky stuff in the hair around my penis."

Not explaining to me that what I had experienced was called a wet dream, my dad seemed suddenly as nervous as I felt. All he could muster himself to say was, "That's natural," as he started to turn and walk out of the room.

I quickly said, "And when I rub my penis, it gets hard and stuff comes out of it."

Now visibly mortified, my dad simply responded with, "You probably shouldn't do that," and promptly walked out of the room leaving me in utter confusion. This one episode served to keep me from asking for help for years afterward. I will say this: after the Lord set me free, I was able to ask my dad why he had been unable to talk with me about sex when I was a boy. His reply? "My dad never talked with me about it, so I didn't know how to talk with you." Makes perfect sense to me now. More on that in a later chapter.

Confusion concerning my identity was exactly the state of mind the enemy would keep me in for years to come. It needs to be said, though, that I take full responsibility for my responses to life—for my choices—even those I felt I had no choice to make.

A BIRTHDAY REVELATION

It takes more than one episode or one circumstance to help shape the perception of a person's own identity, but when it seems every circumstance of his life points to one thing, it becomes difficult to come to any other conclusion. The conclusion that I was not like other boys—that I was different—had become ingrained at a very early age and continued to be reinforced as time went on.

On my twelfth birthday, I got to stay up later than usual and watch TV with my parents. Little did I know as this most wonderful day had begun that it would end with a feeling of utter hopelessness and confusion.

Television was such an amazing invention. Having grown up in the days before color TV—at least in our home—and before the days of the remote control, watching television was a real treat for us. *Flipper* was one of my favorite shows as was another sea adventure show called *Sea Hunt*. I remember having only three channels to choose from, which meant I was often called upon to get up and change the channel for my dad or mom whenever it came time for a favorite family show to come on that required a change to a different network. Sometimes I was even called upon to wiggle the rabbit ears (the antenna) if the signal needed to be made more clear.

Gilligan's Island was absolutely one of my personal favorite shows, and I couldn't wait to get home from school, get my chores done, and watch the latest episode. To this day, I can still recite certain lines, and even a song, from one of my favorite episodes. Television was a powerful tool for me. Watching *The Carol Burnett Show* and *Sonny and Cher* along with *Donnie and Marie* introduced me to a magnificent world of music. I craved shows like *American Bandstand* and *Soul Train* and even thoroughly enjoyed the variety of *The Lawrence Welk Show* and *Hee Haw*.

In addition to the comedy, adventure, and music shows my family watched, we also watched detective/crime shows like *Mannix* and *Hawaii Five-O* and westerns like *Gunsmoke* and *Bonanza*. But during the late '60s and early '70s, the advent of the cutting-edge comedies with social messages began to permeate the culture of our nation and change the way we viewed the world, oftentimes asking us to stretch our own views and question why we believe the way we believe. One such show that probably had the most impact upon my young life was called *All in the Family*.

It featured a family in New York consisting of a patriarch, Archie Bunker; his wife, the ditzy Edith; their daughter, Gloria; and Gloria's liberal husband, Mike (or "Meathead," as Archie so fondly called him). It seemed as if every episode caused much concern with my dad and mom, as they were often reduced to outrage, making comments like, "I can't believe they would talk about such a thing!" or "That's just wrong!" yet finding humor in the situation. I found myself feeling very uncomfortable at times and wondered why only Archie was called a bigot just because he disagreed with his son-in-law. Even though I didn't think the son-in-law was always right, HE was never called a bigot—only the more conservative Archie. It caused me to look up the word, which only caused me more confusion.

According to even today's dictionary, a bigot is "a person who is utterly intolerant of any differing creed, belief, or opinion." It was not lost on me as a child that there was a major amount of hypocrisy going on if a bigot was intolerant because Mike seemed so intolerant of Archie! As an aside, I find it equally confusing today to hear a gay person call me an intolerant bigot and be completely intolerant of me and my differing opinion and experience.

The major reason this show affected me so much was because of the way it portrayed homosexuality as if it were a normal way of life. From my personal experience and very personal involvement in homosexuality, homosexuality was anything but normal! One episode in particular stands out in my mind and has since the day I watched it. Why do I remember the details so vividly? Because of the subject matter, of course, but also because this particular episode aired on my twelfth birthday, February 9, 1971.

Called "Judging Books By Covers," the episode revolves around Archie and a friend he admires named Steve. In this particular installment, Archie's son-in-law, Mike, has a friend that Archie assumes is gay. Mike assures him his friend is not gay but mentions to Archie that his good friend, Steve, just might be. Steve is a bachelor and well respected among the men at Archie's local hangout/bar. Everyone assumes Steve is straight until Archie brings up the conversation he had with his son-in-law. At this point, Steve bares his soul to Archie, telling him he is, indeed, gay. Of course, Archie was made to look foolish and bigoted for daring to have a different opinion than the liberal slant would dictate.

It seemed everyone was talking about this show and this most volatile subject matter. Hearing the venom with which the very conservative men I grew up around condemned the show, and how vile and sickened they felt concerning all things homosexual, I felt very much condemned without ever having been outed at this point in my life. This proved to be yet one more episode in a long series of events in my life that the enemy, the Liar, used to persuade me that I was homosexual. Deep inside, I didn't want to be that way, but everywhere I turned there were little reminders that I was different, that I was something less than a real boy, that I was, indeed, homosexual. Yet, it would take me several more years before I finally gave up all hope of being released from what I considered a prison of my own thoughts about my sexual identity. Though I felt somewhat hopeless, there was still something deep inside me that kept clinging to the hope that maybe, just maybe, one day I would wake up and be like other boys—that I would be changed.

As the dawn of this new reality began to come more and more into focus, I did something I would do from time to time for years to come. That night, I went out into the pasture and looked up into the stars and simply began to cry out to God. "Please change me." Nothing ever seemed to change. Somehow hopeless, yet somehow not.

What a birthday this had turned out to be. Hopeless and confused yet clinging to something I didn't even know whether or not was possible. All I knew was that it seemed each and every circumstance of my life—even the TV shows I watched—pointed to one thing: I was gay.

MY ODD INNER LIFE

If I'm to be completely honest, I considered myself a weird child, even though I tried to present myself outwardly in as "normal" a light as possible. Completely self-focused (which I believe is the grand scheme of the enemy of God—Satan, the Liar), everything I did was very calculated and designed in my mind to make others think as highly of me as possible. In my mind (as the enemy, the Liar, would have it), everyone was talking about me and thinking about me, even when I now know they were not—well, at least not as much as I thought they were. This warped view of reality caused me to re-think and over-think everything in my life. Feeling one has to perform his way through life is one of the most devious schemes of the enemy. Looking back, my inner life was pretty miserable. Self-focus does that to a soul.

Being able to hear a song on the radio and then sit down at a piano and play it seemed to get me teased a lot, so I had to downplay that ability. Being emotionally sensitive made me very aware of the emotional needs of those around me and caused me to be quite sympathetic and compassionate, but again only got me teased by other guys, so at times I would feign toughness that wasn't really me. I could see something and put pencil to paper and render a drawing that looked very realistic. This was one of the few gifts given to me that I don't recall getting teased about except for that one time in first grade. Regardless, the very gifts God had given me to use for

His kingdom, the enemy seemed to be very adept at using to make me feel belittled.

These gifts, the music and the emotional sensitivity, were encouraged by my parents and grandmother Jernigan. Grandma would tell me how blessed I was and how I should not take those gifts for granted, that I should use them for the Kingdom of God. The pressure to conform to my grandmother's vision for my life was just as intense as the pressure to perform so no one would find out what I was truly like—so much so that I felt I could never quite measure up to her or anyone else's expectations. My only recourse? Perform. Yet I disdained performing because of the very thing I craved—attention. See? WEIRD.

When I was about ten years old, the performance dilemma presented itself in a way that still haunts me to this very day. My mom's grandmother Bristol—my great-grandmother—came to our farm to see us. This was the first and only time I recall her coming to our home, as we normally went to visit her in hers. Getting up there in years, she wanted to see her grandchildren and great-grandchildren before travel was completely out of the realm of possibility. We were so excited that she had come to our place to see us where we lived! After a few minutes of pleasantries, my great-grandmother asked me if I could play a song for her on the piano. I froze, wondering how I could possibly get out of the situation. Just as I was about to bolt from the room, my mom and dad, being proud of me, simply said, "Sit down and play your great-grandmother a song."

With all that was in me, I did not want to do it. My parents kindly yet firmly asked me again to sit down and play "just one little song." I refused and ran confused and embarrassed from the room to find some place to hide. The next thing I know, my great-grandmother was saying goodbye. My parents could not hide their disappointment, and they were right to be disappointed. My attitude had been wrong. If I'm to be honest, it was selfish pride that kept me from playing for my great-grandmother. I was more concerned with me and my own feelings than for those of my great-grandmother. And I was more concerned with the fear of failing in my performance—pride—than with the blessing it would have been to her.

A week later, we received the news: my great-grandmother Bristol had died. I remember feeling shock, like a slap of cold water to the face, and then the shock became numbness as the feelings of guilt and shame completely consumed my mind for days and weeks afterward. To this day, I still regret not playing "just one little song" for my great-grandmother. Though I feel forgiven by God, I've found it somewhat more difficult to forgive myself. More on that later.

I'm so grateful for the family God placed me in and allowed me to grow up in. Even though we weren't the most outwardly affectionate family in those days, my mom and dad were very supportive of me in the area of my giftings. They were very encouraging of my musical gifts as well as my ability to draw. What I'm sure must have driven them crazy was my emotional sensitivity. If I felt angry, it was obvious. If I was sad, it was very apparent. If I was hurt, the signs were readily visible. The funny thing is that I was as confused as I'm convinced my parents were! The analogy that describes my constant state of balancing my outward performance with my inward desire to be loved and accepted is the old vaudeville act in which a performer tries to keep multiple plates spinning atop thin wooden dowels. Going from plate to plate, from performance to performance, so people would like me, I found it more and more difficult to keep the "plates" of my life spinning. But somehow I did—for far too many years.

Another aspect that played into my self-view was how needy for attention I was. Like a drug I couldn't get enough of, I had to have all the attention, yet as with my great-grandmother, I also tried to avoid any attention at all. I craved my dad's approval and felt I had to go out of my way to be seen in a good light by him, even though I now know that nothing could have been further from the truth! The problem stemmed from my warped perception of me!

This, in turn, led me to believe that my brothers were vying to take my dad's attention from me and place it squarely upon them. Being the oldest, I guess I felt some divine right as the elder son for all of the attention. With that as the driving force, I made the lives of my little brothers horrible at times, hitting them in anger when they got in my way, teasing them and belittling them (ironic the way the bullied can often become the bully), putting them down in any way I could. That we are now good friends is a testament to God's grace and the forgiveness my brothers have extended toward me since then.

Here's just one example among the countless many. For some reason, this one is seared upon my mind. For all of the years I spent on the farm, each day was pretty much the same. Get up in the morning and tend to the animals before breakfast and before getting ready for school. A farm is hard work and takes everyone pitching in to make the work flow smoothly. One of the favorite things I recall doing with my dad and brothers was haying the cattle because we got to ride on the stack of hay loaded onto the rear lift my dad had built for the tractor. My dad would call out, "Come on, boys! Let's go feed the cows!" Upon hearing those words we would begin our fight for the prime position, the very top of the stack, and would push and shove one another as we ran toward the tractor.

On one particular weekend when I was around six or seven years of age, I heard my dad call out, "Come on, boys! Hay time! Come and help me feed the cows and break the ice on the ponds!" Winter time feeding, while at times cold and miserable, could also be exhilarating and fun. Horses will break the ice on a frozen pond to find their own water. Cattle will not. So, breaking the ice in addition to cutting the wires on the hay bales and scattering the blocks of hay as my dad drove slowly across the pasture was a BIG deal!

As I scurried to find my coat and then scrambled to find my boots, I ran out the back door and headed for the barn just in time to see my dad driving the tractor toward the pasture while my brothers excitedly waved goodbye to me! I ran as quickly as I could, yelling all the while, "Daddy! Wait for me! Daddy, I'm coming!"

Of course, my little brothers had absolutely no intention of alerting my dad to what was going on, and they had every right to keep quiet.

The devastation was very real, and I took it very personally, as if my dad had done this on purpose. Feeling rejected by my dad's perceived rejection and feeling humiliated at the way my brothers had gotten the better of me, I allowed the bitterness that resulted from believing those lies to reduce me to anger and a vengeful heart. My dad did not purposefully reject me or even forget about me; it was I who had to make that leap. My brothers had not rejected me nor did they intentionally try to humiliate me; they were simply being little brothers. Yet because of my need to be accepted and approved of and constantly affirmed, I took it all and made something out of it that was not there, and the enemy, the Liar, won the day.

Never quite able to feel I measured up to my brothers—or ANY other boys—I had quite the bizarre inner life. My self-view? I am one weird, messed-up dude. The saving grace in all of the jumbled mess of my mental life as a child was my grandma Jernigan. She somehow seemed to understand my weirdness and had the most unique way of trying to bring me into a greater awareness of what true reality looks like.

GRANDMA JERNIGAN

There was always so much joy whenever my dad and mom would take me and my brothers to Okmulgee to visit our grandma Jernigan. She had a unique way, as most grandmas do, of making each grandchild feel as if he or she was the most important person in her life at that moment. She lived with her dad, my great-granddad Snyder, in a small wood-frame house. Next to that house was a free-standing garage. What I remember about that old garage is the smell. Having a dirt floor and being constructed of wood, the dampness of the air combined with the aromas of the dirt and wood made for a most wonderful olfactory memory in my mind. To this day, whenever I smell a similar aroma, I'm instantly transported back to that place and those wonderful visits to Grandma's house. When I was about eight or nine years old, my great-granddad Snyder passed away. The next thing I knew, my dad had moved my grandmother Jernigan into a trailer home on our property. This was like heaven to me!

Grandma had a piano. Need I say more? Until that time, I had to look for opportunities to play the piano. My aunt Patsy had one, so I would play it voraciously whenever I got to go see my cousins. And, of course, there was one in the church basement, which I commandeered each and every time we were there—and we were there a lot! In fact, my dad reminded me of the moment he and my mom first realized the extent of my ability to play. Since dad was the song leader at our church, he was the one who conducted choir practice on Wednesday evenings. While the adults were upstairs in the old church building, I'd be downstairs playing away. As they would sing through a song, I'd be listening. As I picked out the melody with my right hand, I'd attempt to match the harmonies I heard using my left hand.

As the choir came to the end of each song, a faint sound of the same song minus vocals could be heard emanating from downstairs. Wondering who was playing the piano downstairs, my parents came down to discover that it was me! It made me so happy that my parents seemed to be very glad about the gift I had somehow kept hidden from them. This somehow made the teasing I often endured at school more bearable. They immediately talked about getting me a piano, but they didn't have to because Grandma had moved next door with hers!

Grandma's trailer home was next to the cow lot and about a hundred feet from the big barn. On the opposite side of her house was a smaller barn where my dad did a lot of repair work and where we kept our pool table. As soon as I got home from school, I'd scramble to get my chores done so I could get to Grandma's house, to that wonderful little piano of hers. She is the one who helped me realize the full potential of harmony and how to properly "chord" a song. Due to my practices at church on Wednesday evenings, I could put feeble chords to a song, but Grandma showed me how to play those same chords in varying inversions and how to break the three note chords up in an arpeggiated style, adding interest to what I was playing, and how the various keys of any given song could be transposed to different keys simply by understanding the mathematical relationship between the different notes and keys. She taught me that the "one" chord and the "four" chord and the "five" chord could be played in ANY key! This revolutionized my ability and made each time at Grandma's piano an absolute adventure of discovery and exploration!

And then, day of all glorious days. Grandma had ordered the Reader's Digest songbook collection, chock full of the standards of yesteryear. She taught me how to play "Has Anybody Seen My Girl" and "The Entertainer" and "The Impossible Dream" and a myriad of songs from the twenties, thirties, and forties. Mind you, I couldn't read the music, but she taught me by playing the song for me once and then encouraging me to follow the ebb and flow—the up and down movement—of the written notes. Hour upon hour upon hour was spent trying to master those old songs. And Grandma would go about her housework while I filled the small trailer with glorious music.

And she would pray for me. More on that later.

More often than not, my grandmother encouraged me to play. As soon as I got home from school, she'd admonish me to get my chores done so I could come to her house. So often were the times I just skipped my chores and went straight to Grandma's house to play, only to hear my mom calling for me. I was the only kid I knew who ever got punished for practicing the piano—ha! Again, I deserved it. It was not too difficult for my mom to find me; all she had to do was listen. If she heard piano music pouring out of Grandma's house, there I was.

In the winter, it was not uncommon for me to be doing my chores in the barnyard next to her house only to see Grandma stick her head out of her back door and call out to me, "Come in here and warm up your hands on the piano when you're done with your chores, son!" I was only too happy to oblige!

I have to tell one funny story about my grandmother Jernigan. Since we lived in what many call Tornado Alley, we often found ourselves watching the weather forecasts of the day and going outside to actually observe the clouds. The most common time for a tornado to occur was in the springtime, but not always. On one summer day when I was about eleven or twelve years old, I was inside our house cleaning the kitchen (I really was, Mom!) while my brother Paul was out doing tractor work in the pasture about a half-mile from home, when I suddenly heard the loudest commotion and the most tremendous sound of wind come up without any warning. Running toward the back door, I came outside just in time to see Dad's repair barn lifting from the earth, turning upside down, and then smashing to the ground in a million shredded pieces. It took me only a second to realize I was seeing a tornado in an up-close and very personal way.

My immediate thought was to run and check on my little brother (really!). Running toward the fence, I didn't even stop to open the gate. I jumped literally OVER the fence and ran with all my might all the way to where my brother was. I flagged him down and asked if he was all right. "What do you mean, am I all right?" he shouted back at me. I said, "The Tornado! Didn't you see the tornado?"

"What tornado?" he yelled.

"The one that destroyed the barn!" I replied.

His next words sent a wave of numbness through my entire being.

"Is Grandma okay?"

Grandma! I had completely forgotten about Grandma Jernigan. Together, my brother and I raced back to Grandma's trailer only to find the front door locked. The trailer seemed to be intact, but we were still very concerned for our grandma. We knocked frantically on the door. It took a few seconds for her to respond. As the door swung open, Grandma caught sight of the demolished barn and said without any hesitation, "What have you boys done?"

After we convinced her that it had indeed been a tornado that was responsible for the destruction, she went on to tell us she had heard a commotion but had simply assumed that Dad's bird dog had simply been dragging his chain against the skirting of her trailer! True story.

Grandma's importance to my life was nearly as immense as the importance of my own parents to me. Grandma was a very spiritually-minded woman. She was Assemblies of God and we were

Southern Baptists—meaning, at times, that it often felt like oil and water around our house whenever anything about church or spiritual things arose in our family's conversations with her. My recollections of that time were simple. To my little-boy mind, God still spoke in her church. In our church, we simply read letters God had written to us. Simple, yet a very accurate belief I held at that time.

My grandmother was instrumental in helping me to develop a basic understanding of the spiritual realm. My parents took me to church and made sure I had an understanding of the gospel, but it was Grandma and her attitude about spiritual depth of reality that intrigued me and helped me to develop what little spiritual sensitivity I was aware of at that time.

Often, she would have me watch Christian television shows with her. She loved the ministry of Oral Roberts and would have me watch his show. So impressed with his ministry was I that I sent away for his very special Prayer Bible. And when I heard the World Action Singers of Oral Roberts University sing, I sent away for their record album! What joy and what a blessing it was to receive those items in the mail. I still have both to this day because they remind me of a precious time of spiritual growth in my life, even if I was completely unaware of what was going on at the time.

On one occasion, Grandma introduced me to the name, Kathryn Kulhman. I'd never heard of her before, but Grandma told me about a special healing crusade she was hosting that was to be televised. I was in awe as this woman of faith would simply wave her hand in a certain direction, and hundreds of people would pass out and collapse to the floor! And still others would come to her for prayer with all manner of physical infirmities, and they would go away rejoicing because God had healed them! I witnessed the lame walking and the blind seeing. I watched as the deaf could suddenly hear, and the mute could suddenly speak. All I knew as a boy was that I wanted to know God like Oral Roberts, like Kathryn Kulhman, like my grandma!

Grandma Jernigan believed she could hear the voice of God when He spoke to her. Many were the times she would tell me things God had spoken to her. One such episode of something God had spoken was so mind-blowing to me that I've never forgotten. She once told me that when she got to heaven she would no longer be married to my granddad Jernigan because there was no need. She went on to tell me how Jesus Himself had confirmed this to her through the reading of Matthew 22:30 NASB, which simply says, "For in the resurrection they neither marry nor are given in marriage, but are like angels in heaven." He died when I was only one year old, so I never really knew him, but she'd tell me about him.

She told me she had simply asked the Lord how she would know my grandfather once she went to be with the Lord. She whispered to me what the Lord spoke to her. She spoke in such a reverent, awe-inspiring tone that I remember getting goose bumps. "When I get to heaven, the first thing I'm going to do is spend time worshiping Jesus. And then, I'm going to call out the new name God gave your grandfather Jernigan. In that way, I will recognize him."

I still remember the name she told me, and I'll keep it hidden in my heart until the day I get to heaven. Since I cannot recall being with my grandfather—although I've seen pictures of him holding me (they tell me he carried me everywhere with him around town, bragging on me to whoever would listen!)—I'll simply do what Grandma told me. I'll call out his new name and spend time with him after I've spent some time worshiping Jesus!

Grandma Jernigan's home—Grandma's arms, attitude, and love—was a refuge for me in so many ways. Countless hours beating out my frustrations on her piano. Countless admonishments from her to use my talents for the One who had given them to me. Countless blessings upon blessings of the many memories I now treasure because of who she was. And then she was gone. And I was devastated.

A few weeks before she died, Grandma had taken me aside and told me her wishes for her funeral. She sensed it would be someday in the near future. I just remember being in denial yet wanting to please Grandma, so I listened. She gave me a list of Scriptures she wanted read at her funeral service. She handed me a stack of music she wanted sung at her funeral. She told me that the funeral was for us, her family, and that the Lord had shown her exactly what verses we would need to hear and had revealed to her exactly which songs to have sung that would minister to us. She was completely unselfish.

I heard the phone ring about 3:30 AM, and then I heard my dad's footsteps downstairs as he stumbled to the phone. Only a few days before, my grandmother had been admitted to the hospital in Tulsa. She had been diagnosed with cirrhosis of the liver, which was shocking to us since she'd never taken one drink of alcohol in her entire life. I heard my dad answer the phone and begin to sob. I'd never seen nor had I heard my father cry before that night. To hear him in uncontrollable, inconsolable sobs scared me. At the same time, it broke my heart that my grandmother, for all I know, had been alone when she died. Yet, I knew she was looking into the face of Jesus at that moment, and I imagined she'd already called out the new name my grandfather was known by in heaven, the one the Spirit had whispered to her just a few months before.

The very next day, her pastor came to our house to meet with my dad to discuss funeral plans. Without hesitation, I went to the place I'd hidden Grandma's funeral plans and carried them downstairs. Interrupting their meeting, I simply said, "Here are Grandma's plans for her funeral. She's taken care of everything. Here are the songs. Here are the Scriptures she wants read. This is what she wanted to do to minister to us." And I walked out of the room as my dad and the pastor sat there in stunned silence.

Being awkwardly thirteen, I was so self-conscious at the funeral. Having been so close to Grandma, I took her death very personally, like I was the only one affected by it. Numb from the loss, I sat there while those songs were sung and stared blankly into space while the verses were read. But then the words to Grandma's song for the family shook me to awareness and the stark reality that she was really gone.

I WANT TO STROLL OVER HEAVEN WITH YOU

If I surveyed all the good things that come to me from above
If I could count all the blessings from the storehouse of love
I'd simply ask for the favor of Him beyond mortal end
And I'm sure He would grant it again and again
I want to stroll over Heaven with you some glad day
When all the troubles and heartaches are truly vanished away
Then we'll enjoy the beauty where all things are new
I want to stroll over Heaven with you

So many places of beauty we long to see here below
But time and treasures have kept us from making plans as
    you know
But come the morning of rapture together we'll be
I want to stroll over Heaven with you
I want to stroll over Heaven with you some glad day
When all the troubles and heartaches are truly vanished away
Then we'll enjoy the beauty where all things are new
I want to stroll over Heaven with you

We'll renew old acquaintance with the friends we once knew
Then we'll meet all our loved ones and meet Jesus, too
That will be a glad reunion and there'll be much to view
While I stroll over heaven with you
I want to stroll over Heaven with you some glad day
When all the troubles and heartaches are truly vanished away
Then we'll enjoy the beauty where all things are new
I want to stroll over Heaven with you[1]

The song brought me much solace, but then we drove to the cemetery. As I headed to the family car with my brothers and

---

[1] Words & Music by Milton A. Dodson, © 1956 Dodson Music Co. Used by permission.

parents, it was discovered there was not room for all of us, so I was instructed to ride with my aunt and uncle. I was mortified. Didn't everyone know how close I was to Grandma? Didn't everyone realize what a slight it was for me to not be riding in the family car? It's not easy for me to now see just how self-focused I'd become. The enemy had set me up once again. No one was slighting me. If anything, they were honoring me by deeming me mature enough to not have to ride with the little ones—that I was strong enough to handle this alone.

As the cars pulled onto the highway, I sat in the back seat of my aunt and uncle's car and sobbed all the way to the cemetery. I vowed then and there I would not get close to anyone ever again because it hurt too much to lose them. Even though I went into a shell emotionally, God would continue to use the things He had taught me through my grandmother Jernigan to eventually bring deep healing to my broken heart.

JOY IN THE MIDST OF PAIN

From what you've read of my story thus far, you may be thinking of how miserable my existence must've been, but that is far from the truth. Through moments of pain and of joy, I've learned that we can focus on the negative, or we can focus on the positive. Since I tend to be a glass half-empty kind of guy, it's taken me a bit more effort to get to the place of being a glass half-full guy, but it's been worth it. What I've discovered in the process is that God will waste nothing—not even our sorrows, failures, or wounds— if we will but bring them to Him in honesty and ask Him to show us HIS point of view in each circumstance.

Even though my life was full of hidden hurts and constant turmoil, life was quite the adventure. As I look back, I'm actually astonished at all God allowed me to enjoy, even in the midst of my tormented existence as a young man. It's easy now to see that during so much of my younger life, I was simply sitting underneath the table settling for the crumbs while all along, God had a feast prepared for me. He was actually calling me to come and sit AT the table WITH Him in the presence of my enemies! Talk about an adventure! Life and its many wonders have continued to grow within the far reaches of my soul to such an extent that I can actually thank God for all I've gone through to get to the place of intimate relationship with Him.

As a family, we spent many weekends in the summer at a place called Horseshoe Bend on the Illinois River, near Tahlequah, Oklahoma. Fishing and exploring were the number one issues on my mind in those days. I remember wild hogs getting into our food and my dad having to hide it in wooden, locked boxes. I recall my mama making breakfast every morning and frying fish every evening. Oh, how those aromas take me back to pleasant memories even to this day.

My parents would drive us several miles upriver and drop us off with nothing but our inner tubes, allowing us to float for hours all the way back to camp. Many hours were spent jumping and diving from the banks and from the many rope swings we would encounter along the way. One time, we even took turns curling up inside a tractor inner tube and rolling off the banks and into the river. From the time I was a little boy I dreamed of one day swimming across the river by myself. I still remember the exhilaration and sense of accomplishment I felt the first time I did it. From hanging out with my brothers and cousins to playing horseshoes and crazy eights with my parents by lantern, these times of family togetherness went a long way in keeping me sane during a very trying time in my life.

Another diversion from the heaviness of same-sex attraction that I felt as a boy was my love for horses. My first pony was named Spot. Spot was hit by a car on the highway in front of our home and was killed. This happened when I was about four years old. While I recall feeling VERY sad, I also remember wanting another horse. Daddy bought a Shetland pony from my uncle. Being a Lone Ranger fan, we called the little feisty pony Silver. I remember how proud I was the day my dad saddled up Silver then saddled up his big horse, Chico, and told me to follow him through the pasture and into the open gate of our neighbor's land. Riding into the field, he led me to a freshly dug pit—a brand new pond—and then into the still-dry canyon and called for me to follow him. I've never forgotten the awe

I felt at my dad's trust—that he considered me big enough to ride my own horse behind him, and not just behind him on his!

Next, Daddy bought me a Welsh pony that we called Robin. Robin was one of the most gentle horses I've ever known. My brothers and I got the bright idea one day to see if Robin could pull our little red wagon if we attached a rope to her saddle horn. And she could! For years, it was not uncommon to see the Jernigan boys out speeding across the pasture, one boy riding Robin while the other three crowded into the wagon. Over bumps and around and through and over the pasture we sped, our favorite obstacle being the many terraces that went with the contour of the land (built in the 1930s to help conserve topsoil and prevent erosion). Over these bumps we would fly, often going airborne in the process. If we crashed and burned, the more we laughed. We did this so many times we would wear the wagon to shreds, the handle and front wheels ripping right away from the undercarriage of the wagon! Many were the times my dad had to weld those wheels back on.

One of our favorite pastimes on horseback was simply exploring the countryside. In the summertime, you could find my brothers, my cousins, and me somewhere on horseback. Our adventures often took us through miles and miles of countryside as we explored the many creeks winding through the hills and meadows. We knew seemingly every place within a ten-mile radius where we could negotiate a horse in or through, and we would ride from sunup 'til sundown. We would play hide-and-seek on horseback. We would play tag on horseback. We would play cowboys and Indians on horseback, always fighting over who got to be the Indians because we thought they were so cool.

During one particular summer, my mother kept wondering why my brothers, cousins, and I always seemed so clean after being out riding horses all day. Little did she know that before our daily rides ended, we would make our way to the big back pond, where we would skinny-dip until we were tuckered out. That all ended the day my dad and uncle decided to take the pickup truck, with all my girl cousins in the back, to check the back pasture. We didn't see them coming until it was too late. There, careening around the corner of the pond bank, came the truck full of laughing and screaming girls!

Of course, we tried to hide under the water but could only hold our breath for so long. It didn't dawn on me until later that, even if we could've hidden indefinitely underwater, our clothes hanging over the fence and our horses tied next to them were a dead giveaway as to our bare activities. My dad simply stopped the truck and asked us what we thought we were doing. Of course it was quite obvious, but he went on to say, "Get your tails to the house!"

As soon as the truck and girls were out of sight, we fearfully made our way to our clothes and our horses and took as much time as we could getting back home. We all just knew that a spanking awaited us once we were there. And sure enough, my dad and my uncle were there waiting. As they took off their belts to give us our due punishment, my grandmother Jernigan interceded. Speaking to my dad, she merely said, "Wait a minute there. Don't you dare! I seem to recall YOUR skinny white butt running along that same pond bank when you were their age!" My dad and uncle just laughed and put their belts back on, never truly intending to spank us. We were much more careful about our naked adventures from that time on.

How I loved my horses and the time I was able to spend on their wondrous backs. My absolute favorite memory of the many horses I owned was my horse, Sugar, and the weekly rides we made into town from our farm. My cousins would often ride their horses over to our house. We would then all take burlap bags—we called them tow sacks—and ride down the sides of the highway the three miles into town, picking up glass pop bottles along the way. Once in town, we would sell our bottles in the hopes of having enough money for a burger and a pop—and we usually did have. God used such times to build hope and joy into my life, even though it seemed the enemy had a way of robbing me of that very hope and joy.

As a boy, I had a need for finding ways of escape from the emotional turmoil and anguish of my struggle with same-sex attraction. Of course I could "get away from it all" at the piano when I was at home, and I could get away when on my horse, but what about the times at school where most of the trauma was experienced? I don't recall what year I discovered books, but it was around my third-grade year that my teacher introduced me to the Scholastic Book Club. Once a month, she'd hand out the most amazing flyers from this company, and within its wondrous pages were pictures of book covers along with descriptions of what each book was about.

It didn't take me long to discover the amazing stories of Marguerite Henry. Within those pages I could be transported from ocean to mountain, from pony to wild mustang, within a matter of only a few chapters. What wild adventures and mad escapes these were for me. I read voraciously. *Misty of Chincoteague, Justin Morgan Had a Horse, King of the Wind, Brighty of the Grand Canyon,* and *Stormy, Misty's Foal* were all consumed. And then I discovered the writings of Jack London and found myself transported to the northern climes of the Klondike and the most incredible journeys within the pages of *The Call of the Wild* and *White Fang.* Reading took me to places of incredible pain but always transported me safely within the comfort of my own soul and somehow gave me hope that maybe, just maybe, I would make it through life just like the heroes of my books had done.

Even though I found it more and more difficult to believe anyone could possibly love me if they knew what I was truly like, I know now that my perceptions were quite skewed. Whether we like it or not, life, with its many twists and turns and its many hurtful circumstances, has a way of causing us to become so inwardly focused that we (at least I did) begin to feel more like a victim than a victor. My parents were ALWAYS there for me, but because of my own warped perception, they seemed so distant. All I have to do is look back and see all they provided in the way of stability, and I'm quickly brought humbly to my knees in thanksgiving that God caused me to be born within the family I was born into. I shudder to think what my life would've been like had my dad and mom not worked so hard to provide a safe and loving home for us boys.

They made adventure easy and accessible to me, and there is much to be said for that. By providing a place of security for me and encouraging me to take risks, they were actually setting me up for the greatest adventure of my life—the battle for my own freedom; the adventure of the long, dark nights my soul would encounter along the way; and always, ALWAYS reminding me (even if I could never quite believe I was worthy of it) that as long as they were here, I would have a safe place to find refuge and comfort.

It would be many years before that adventure of freedom would be realized. There was still high school.

I LIKE DREAMING

From the time I was about ten years old, and after overhearing the men of my church, whom I respected so much, talking about what they thought of homosexuals, I felt trapped—like I had suddenly become aware that I was imprisoned within my own mind with no way of escape. Mental confusion ruled the day and caused a deep longing for someone to sweep in and rescue me. I didn't realize it at the time, but I was developing the mental attitude of a victim—that somehow everything that was happening to me was someone else's fault. As I look back, it's easy to see that even in dire circumstances, I always had the power of choice, to choose how I would respond.

Puberty hit me with all its fury when I was eleven, only causing more confusion as to who I was and what it meant to be a male, a man. What sent me cleanly over the edge and into the realm of inner madness was the death of my grandmother Jernigan when I was thirteen. Whether I knew how to communicate it or not, I was in utter self-preservation mode. My outward life continued in very calculated performance mode while my inner life felt utterly out of control. I longed daily for someone to somehow rescue me from all the madness.

Being labeled a sissy by the older boys at such an early age had quite a profound effect on my psyche. As I look back, I don't think I would change a thing, though. I know that sounds crazy, but

I don't believe I would be where I am today. I wouldn't have the depth of understanding of my true identity nor the depth of intimacy with my God I now enjoy had I not endured all I went through. That is truly a Kingdom of God point of view—that even though bad things happen, God is in control and will use those things meant for evil against us for our very own good!

In actuality, the teasing from those early years only intensified as the years went by. In fact, the same boy who had attacked me that first time on the playground continued his taunting and harassing behavior all the way through high school. In addition, he had recruited several other boys to his cadre of tormentors. Like minions of evil torture, this small group of boys seemed to live only to make me as miserable as possible. I dreaded going to school. If I could make it to where my friends were without being cornered by this group of boys, I considered it a successful start to the school day.

Our school was small. We averaged about seventy-five students in the entire high school, grades nine through twelve, so everyone knew everyone. Even in a small school, cliques develop around commonalities like race and interests. Even though the school was racially diverse—almost evenly split between black and white—there were not many racial problems when I was in school. My reality was that I tended to identify more with the black kids than with the redneck kids, and that proved to be quite the problem for me at times. It was my common practice to look up and down the hallway between classes in order to gauge my best route to the next class that would help me avoid my tormentors.

Being raised on a farm in a small farming community and being from a small school, most of our choices in class subjects were very limited. I took one year of algebra (which mystifies me to this day) and several vocational agriculture courses. I was in 4-H in grade school and segued into Future Farmers of America (FFA) once I was in high school. I loved my agriculture teacher, Gene Ross, and learned to weld and judge land and judge cattle and write speeches on soil conservation and the like under his tutelage. As I think of myself now, I was Napoleon Dynamite long before the advent of that comedic character!

It was as if I lived in two diametrically opposite and polar opposite worlds—the world of basketball and my black friends who readily embraced me, and the world of vocational agriculture and the rednecks who despised me. The rednecks made it very apparent that they detested me. Even though some of my black friends took vo-ag courses as well, there was little they could do to protect me most of the time. It seemed a common thing for me to get cornered by the rednecks whenever none of my black friends were around.

Remember Lonnie, the bully from my grade school days? He grew up. He called me Bullhead most often, mixed with the regular names of fag and queer, but never my name. And all his little cronies would do the same. The dirty little secret was that one of his minions was actually one of my sexual partners. When this boy was alone with me, I was his best friend whom he used sexually, yet this same boy would join right in the choruses of teasing with Lonnie and the others, leaving me too afraid to respond lest he "out" me. Never once did I even consider "outing" him. Fear saw to that. I was one twisted young man.

I was one of the only white kids in our high school choir. I was a starter on the basketball team, the only white boy on the team at times throughout my high school career. I got a lot of attention both on and off the court because of the stark juxtaposition of being the only white face in a sea of brown. Two of the older African American boys, Stevie and Lawrence, would affectionately and playfully call me "Black Boy". I loved it. Such kind words, even in jest, were signs of the acceptance and approval I craved. But once the white boys got wind of this, I was labeled a nigger lover. And I hated that word. Of course, the white boys never called me that when any of my black friends were around—only when they had me alone and cornered and defenseless. It seems they were braver in numbers when it came to teasing me. I'd never thought of that until I committed these words to the page. I don't recall getting teased by any one boy by himself; it was always when groups of two or more came against me. Curious.

Of course, being the only white boy on my team at times led to some very confrontational moments for me as well. We played a lot of schools that were all white, and we played yet other teams that were all black. I sort of stuck out! To make matters worse, we had a stellar defense, playing full court press from the start of many games. I, being the point of that press, made it my goal to trap the opposing team member between me and my teammate and cause him to lose control or lose possession of the ball. I was like a gnat on the court, flying around getting in the face of the enemy and trying to steal the ball. At other times we played teams that had one strong player, and I was often assigned to him in a box-one defense. My four teammates played a zone defense while I stuck to the opposing star player like glue, with the goal of causing him to foul me. In four years as a starter, I fouled out only one time. My point?

I made the life of the opposing player so miserable at times that I caused him to lash out in frustration at me, bumping me and threatening to hit me. During such moments, I had so much confidence I'd simply fold my arms and say, "Go ahead! You're about to make the biggest mistake of your life!" Why was I so confident? Because I knew that once my teammates saw the confrontation, they would surround me and protect me, come to my defense. These were the same hopes I had for my inner life as well, that someone would surround me and protect me and come to my defense. Even though that never seemed to happen for me concerning my inner life, God was using the outward circumstances of my life to paint a very vivid picture of what He was already doing for me and trying to do in me.

With the advent of television and the world of adventure it opened up to me, coupled with the books I read, I longed for adventure. That longing, together with my need for someone to rescue me from my hopeless existence, caused me to become enthralled with a new TV show of the era called *Lost in Space*. I used to become so involved in the plots of the series that I would imagine myself being the main child protagonist, Will. Not only did I imagine what life was like for Will, but I imagined at times that I WAS Will.

But then an even more wonderful show was introduced to my fantasy world of adventure—*Star Trek*! I LOVED *Star Trek*. I would think about it all day long. What would life on the Enterprise be like for a boy? What would I do if I was on the bridge? What would I say to Scotty or Sulu or Uhura or Bones or Spock? What if Captain Kirk was my dad? What would life be like then? So deep was my love of all things *Star Trek* that my dreams at night became consumed with the adventure I experienced beyond just watching the show.

As soon as I got home from school each day, I'd rush to get my chores done, have supper with my family, and then go right to the piano my parents had bought for me after my grandmother Jernigan had passed away. Music was my escape during the evening, but dreams were my escape throughout the night. As soon as my head hit the pillow, I was suddenly and magically transported aboard the USS Enterprise. My dad was Captain James Tiberius Kirk. Each night, from the time I was about ten years old until well after I had graduated from college, I dreamed the same dream.

As was often the case on the TV show, there were many alien life forms that were out for my demise. Each night I would be captured by these aliens. Their plan was always to put me to death to punish my dad, Captain Kirk. Just as they were about to put me to death, my dad would suddenly materialize with his phaser set not on "stun" but on "destroy." With one decisive pull of the trigger and with precision aim, my dad would summarily put the aliens down just as I woke up!

My mom in my dreams was Doris Day, and I would wake up hearing the words to her signature song, "Que sera, sera. Whatever will be, will be. The future's not ours to see. Que sera, sera." Every morning for years I woke up feeling rescued and at the same time feeling I must be going insane to have the same dream night after night, year after year. Looking back, it's quite easy to see how much the Lord loved me and how much He was trying to communicate hope and assurance to me that rescue was indeed on the way. As a young boy and young man, I just didn't have the spiritual depth or awareness to see it at the time. But in my memory, I now find deep joy and am deeply overwhelmed at the extent God went to, to get that message to me.

I remember thinking, "If I can get through the school day, if I can get to basketball practice, if I can just get home and get my chores done and get to the piano, then no one can touch me, especially in my dreams. During my high school days and beyond, that was my existence. God used it all to develop what I call a giant killer's attitude, even if I didn't feel like a giant killer at the time. You see, God wasted nothing, not even my despair, not even my loneliness, not even my dreams, not even my failure, and there was plenty of that.

On one summer evening when I was fifteen years old, I spent the night with a friend. During that night, a family member came home after having been gone for many years. This man was at least twenty years older than me and seemed to be well loved by the family. After just a few minutes, it was obvious that he was a humorous man who loved to laugh and tease, but in a loving way, if that makes sense. His teasing, even though he didn't know me, came across as endearing, like we suddenly had an inside joke between two long-lost friends. I genuinely liked being around him, especially since he was much older and wiser in the ways of the world than I. He was a very manly man, something that attracted me to him right away because I so longed to be like that.

During the night, I was sleeping on the couch. As it happened, the house was small and the bedrooms full, so this family friend simply made a pallet on the floor and proceeded to sleep in the living room just a few feet from where I was asleep. As the night wore on, I awoke for some reason. As I lay there, I could hear this man moving around, restless. And then I heard him speak. "Are you awake?"

I quietly said, "Yes."

The next thing I knew, he was standing there naked in front of me, exposing himself to me. Though dark in the room, there was enough light coming in from the moonlit night to allow me to see that he was becoming quite aroused. Without saying a word, he took me by the arm and led me to his sleeping area and had me lie down with him. There is no need for me to share any more details than that. The reason I share is because this was the first time I'd been with someone sexually who I didn't consider a peer, someone near my age. The effect it had on me was tremendous because this man didn't have any of the outward effeminate qualities I had associated with homosexuality up to that point. My perspective suddenly changed. ANYONE might be gay! Talk about confusion! I no longer had any semblance of an anchor with which to secure my thoughts. That night I crossed into a realm I was totally unprepared for, a realm that would ravage my life in ways I could never have imagined. Like being stranded in a barren wilderness or on a planet where there was no other life form whatsoever, I felt so utterly alone with no way out.

At least I could dream.

ONWARD AND DEEPER
INTO THE ABYSS

Somehow, even in the midst of non-stop ridicule and teasing from that small group of boys, I managed to survive high school. Despite all the inner turmoil, I really did have many happy memories. Who gets to play in three state high-school basketball tournaments? Who gets to be a State Farmer in FFA? Who gets to win the county 4-H speech contest? Who gets to spend hours on horseback and hours fishing 'til their heart's content? Who gets to go camping with their parents and siblings? Who gets to grow up with their cousins? Who gets to have both a mom and a dad who support you, even if they don't understand you? Yet, it is true that the underlying current of my inner life did cloud everything to a certain degree.

Throughout high school, I only had what I would consider three steady girlfriends. One relationship lasted less than a week, but it did result in my first kiss—as a junior. Another relationship lasted a few weeks, while the one I was most serious about lasted several months. While I thought each of the girls was physically beautiful, I had no sexual attraction to them. But I thought that by going out with them, by making out with them, I would change. Nothing ever happened because I never felt any response whatsoever "down there." I just kept hoping and praying that one day "it" would start working.

Another factor that kept me somewhat pure in my relationships with the opposite sex is that I'd been taught by my mom to respect women. In addition, because I was such good friends with most of the girls I knew, I heard all the stories of how they felt used by other guys, and I never wanted to be "that" guy. Even though I had make-out sessions with those three girls, I never felt confident enough to even attempt anything beyond kissing, and I didn't want them to feel used—which is funny because used is how I ALWAYS felt with other guys.

My senior year brought with it many opportunities and accolades— at least as far as a small-town school and its small-town opportunities could afford. Our state representative invited me to serve as a page in the state House of Representatives. This was such an honor for me because I'd never really ventured outside the realm of basketball or FFA in my school activities. For one whole week, I was privileged to get a glimpse into the workings of our state government. Most of the people I dealt with during that week were from small towns like mine, yet it was easy to tell from talking with the other students that we all had dreams of a bigger world awaiting us out there.

Scared to death is how I'd describe myself as I faced high school graduation. Giving the valedictory speech was the most monumental moment for me— partly because my dad had been valedictorian of HIS graduating class from the same school and partly because it was seen as such a tremendous honor. I had no clue as to what I would do after graduation, but my parents really wanted me to consider going to college, meaning I would be the first one in our family to EVER go to college. Talk about a huge burden. And talk about stepping out into the unknown! My parents couldn't help me get ready since neither of them had gone to college. For the first time, I realized I'd be on my own— that life would be up to ME.

One of the first steps I made in setting out into that world was to visit Oklahoma Baptist University. Growing up Baptist meant I received a lot of promotional materials from that university and felt much pressure to attend, both self-inflicted and otherwise. During a visit to campus, I wanted to kill three birds with one stone: I would try out for the basketball team, I would audition for a music scholarship, and I would get a feel for whether or not I belonged there.

I was beyond fearful as I walked out onto the basketball court and greeted the assistant coach. He told me he was going to have me scrimmage with the second team and that we would play the first team! My fear only heightened as each player walked up and shook my hand, and I kept having to look higher and higher just to make eye contact! Never had it dawned on me that I was short at 5 feet 11 inches! I was reminded of how I used to ask God to make me 6 feet 5 inches tall, but He never did (Oh, how I wished He had!).

The scrimmage went very well. I was able to keep up with the fast-paced practice and actually anticipated several passes in time to step out and make steals. I can't recall whether I made a bucket or not. All I remember is the coach walking up to me and saying, "You did really well, Dennis. Right now I've got several players ahead of you with a bit more talent and a bit more experience, so I can't offer you a scholarship. If you'd like, I can speak with the local junior college and probably get you a scholarship there. That'll give you two years to grow and mature in your play, and then I'd invite you back for another tryout. If you choose not to do that, I'd welcome you to this team, but you'd have to come in as a walk-on."

Looking into the junior college, I soon realized they had no music department to speak of, and since my goal was to get a music degree, I'd have to decline the offer to attend there. I called the coach later that summer and told him of my desire to walk on with the program. He was happy to allow me to do so, but I would soon quit the team before the first practice ever took place. More on that in a bit.

After my basketball tryout, I went to the music auditions. Since I would be trying out for both a piano and vocal scholarship, I simply prepared to sing a song I had often sung in church back in Boynton. I sang "For Those Tears I Died" and another song called "Little Flowers Never Worry." I felt so proud of myself because I played and sang those songs flawlessly, even though the judges seemed to have bewildered looks of sympathy on their faces. I assumed they had been so moved by my performance, they felt deep compassion. It never dawned on me that perhaps that was not exactly what the professors conducting the auditions were looking for until they invited me to sit in and watch another audition. As the would-be student walked in, he handed his sheet music to the accompanist. Announcing he would be singing "Caro mio ben" by Tommaso Giordani, the pianist began playing the song, and the student began singing the song in the most beautiful tone and with the most precise posture. It was the most proper manner I had ever seen—like an opera singer!

Mortified that I was the most complete rube/hick/country bumpkin they must've ever seen, I slinked out of the room and walked to the piano audition just in time to hear the student trying out just before me playing the most intricate classical melody I had ever heard. I thought to myself, "THAT'S what they want?!" I was almost too embarrassed to even go on with the audition, so numb was I with humiliation. The next thing I know, the voice of the piano professor was asking me, "And what selection will you be playing for us today, Mr. Jernigan?" As my face turned an even brighter red, I informed them I would be playing "For Those Tears I Died" by Marsha Stevens and "Little Flowers Never Worry" by Beth Barnard. At least I had already learned the proper audition etiquette of announcing the song title and composer. After playing the first song, I prepared to launch into the second one, but the professor stopped me, saying, "That's good, Mr. Jernigan. We've heard all we need to hear. You'll be hearing from us within a week as to whether or not you will receive a scholarship."

After the humiliation of those auditions, the enemy began to have a heyday with me, taking my mind to the depths of self-loathing and self-despising thought. My impression, as I then toured the campus with the student leader assigned to usher me around, was that everyone was talking about me and pointing at me and whispering things like, "There's that hick! Can you believe the songs he sang for his audition? or "Look at him! He thought he was so good until he saw what real music sounded like!" I didn't remember much about the campus tour because all I could think of was in getting the heck out of there and back home and never showing my humiliated face in those parts again!

Somehow I summoned up the courage to pack up my things at the end of that summer. My parents didn't go with me to help me move in to the dorm. My cousin, Donna, went with me. Had it not been for her, I never would've had the courage to step one foot on that campus. I packed my 1960 Ford Galaxie 500 (a seventeen-year-old car that I had bought from my dad) with everything I owned, and my cousin followed me in her car so she could drive home after helping me unload. I'll never forget the sweeping fear of dread that overtook my being as I watched her drive away.

My first roommate was an upperclassman, a senior. That lasted all of one week when he told me he needed to move in with a friend whose roommate had just told him he wasn't coming back to school. Of course, I felt rejected even though his story was probably true. My next roommate was a fellow freshman with whom I'm still friends to this day. Well groomed and handsome, I immediately sensed a huge difference between us. Dewey had grown up in a large city, and it was obvious by his possessions that his family was more prosperous than ours. From day one, I never felt I measured up to Dewey—or to anyone.

And then there were the awkward morning rituals of shaving and showering. I had never been naked in a locker room with other guys—ever. And now to be thrust into a situation where, in an all-male dorm, it was not uncommon to see completely naked men walking from their dorm room to the shower room—and once in the shower room, to see multiple naked men. Having no frame of reference for this new reality, I was immediately tempted to stare. I was a skinny country boy with little body hair among seemingly an army of hairy, macho, uninhibited beasts. A boy among real men. Temptation took hold of me often, but I kept telling myself to simply look down and do my thing and get out of there as quickly as possible. My fear? An unwanted erection! The fear of other men seeing me aroused was enough to keep me from getting aroused, thank God! Those locker room encounters would tempt me with unwanted same-sex attraction and yet toughen me to keep my sexual attraction to men to myself.

That first week of school was merely an introductory week of getting to know the ins and outs of university life as well as getting to know other students. But in my mind, it was a monumental effort by some unseen force of the universe to make me feel as humiliated as ever. The fact that I even endured that week is quite a miracle to me. My haircut was dated and countrified, according to the styles most of the other guys were wearing. My clothes were outdated and looked as if I was going to a rodeo. I had nothing in common with most of the other students since most of them seemed to have come from big cities and large, sophisticated high schools. And to top it all off, we had to wear these ridiculous beanies that signified our positions as "lowly freshman" as we were told to address ourselves to upper classmen.

Once school began and actual classroom work was underway, most of the humiliation of that first week was easily forgotten. Because I had such an affinity for music, a good ear, they placed me in the Music Theory B—of four classes, the next to the highest! After one semester, they placed me in Music Theory A because I had made so much progress. More on that later.

To be a music major in those days, one was required to be part of a choral group on campus each semester. And how does one become part of a choral group? One must audition, of course. And here's how my audition went. "Mr. Jernigan, will you please take that choral octavo, go to the second page and to the third score, and read the alto line in your register?" They might as well have been speaking Russian. I had absolutely no idea what they had just asked me to do!

I failed the audition, obviously. But never fear, they had a "special" choir for guys like me. They called it the Shawnee Choral Society. Whenever someone would ask me what choir I had been placed in, I would mumble as quietly as possible, "Shawnee Choral Society," to which they would respond with great pity, "Aww, that's okay." I was so embarrassed by this new identity and life-sentence that I gave the choir another name: The Island of Misfit Toys!

But wait, there's more—humiliation, that is. Remember those days I told you about when I would sit at grandma Jernigan's piano and play for hours? It was quite common for me to make up my own songs, even as a boy, though I never knew how to write any of them on a musical score. When we were asked by our student advisers what we would like our specific music major to be, I told them I wanted to write, to compose. I felt it was in me to do so.

My adviser sent me to the head of the Theory and Composition department, telling me I must first apply for a position in that department. Sitting across the desk from the department head, I announced, "I want to write music. I would like to major in composition." Her response without hesitation? "We have only a few positions in this department, and we reserve them for people we see potential in. We simply do not see any such potential in you. Based on your auditions and abilities demonstrated thus far, I must say no."

I felt I had nowhere to turn for help. In my pride, I couldn't risk telling others in the same music classes that I felt inferior, that I had not had music lessons as many of them had while growing up. I even feared telling my parents. Not wanting them to think I couldn't hack it and not wanting them to be put in the position of telling me what to do in a situation they had never been privileged to experience, not wanting them to feel inferior as I now felt, I felt so very alone.

I was crushed. I constantly felt humiliated, whether real or imagined. I was constantly longing to reach out to others, but no one seemed open to a countrified hick like me. Besides, I had no experience in real relationship with other males. Yet I longed for—craved—male attention. The years of taunting and teasing and humiliation I had endured while a boy now seemed amplified and intensified beyond my ability to compensate for or perform my way through. This only led to a deeper longing for intimacy and male attention and was the perfect setup for a long, downward spiral into the belief that I was without hope—that I was indeed homosexual. Soon enough, I would find other young men who felt the same way, and that would not be a good thing.

ENCOUNTERS

My freshman year saw me having to learn how to negotiate the ins and outs of the simplest things. I'd never applied for a school loan and had never had to go from department to department to enroll in classes. Being an artistic soul, such tedious endeavors were torture for me. In addition, trying to come to grips with the musical terminology being hurled at me was like being thrust into a room in which everyone but me spoke Russian! Most of the time that first semester, I didn't have a clue as to what was going on. It wasn't until after Thanksgiving that things began to make any sense to me, but when they did, I took off!

Sight singing was the most intimidating thing I had encountered. At least with the theoretical things, as they applied to musical notation, I could eventually decipher, but looking at a series of spots on lines left me completely bewildered. Whenever the teacher would ask us to sing a couple of measures by sight, I tried to duck down behind someone, which is not easily done in a class of about fifteen students! After I caught on to the idea that she was assigning a numerical place to each note in the scale, it began to make sense to me. It didn't take me long, though, to apply what I heard to what I saw. An interval between 1 and 4, a perfect fourth, sounded like "Here Comes the Bride," and the interval between a 1 and a 3 in a minor scale sounded like the beginning of "Beethoven's Ninth Symphony!" In other words, I did whatever I could to get by.

But, thank God, my understanding of music theory finally did begin to kick in. So much so, that after testing at the end of the first semester, I was bumped from the B Theory class into the A theory class, with the legendary Katherine Timberlake. Her reputation was one of intensity and precision; she did not tolerate silliness of any sort. Scared to death by all the stories I'd heard about her, I entered her class with much fear and trembling. Whenever I told anyone I was going to be in her theory class, the response was always a mocking, high-pitched mimicry of Mrs. Timberlake: "Keep the beat! Keep the beat!" I anticipated being cast away from her presence the moment I couldn't "keep the beat."

What I found, though, was quite the opposite. From day one in her class, my impression was one of deep respect and honor because it became quickly apparent that she wanted nothing but the best from her students and was trying to lead us to excellence. Rather than brow-beating her students as I'd expected, I found her to be one of the most encouraging teachers I'd ever encountered. Was she tough? Yes! Was she intolerant of laziness? You bet! Would I do it all over again if I had to face her in class once more? Absolutely. What I gained from that wonderful lady was to profoundly affect my life far beyond my scholastic studies. She helped equip me for song writing in ways I'm forever grateful. Thanks to her, I can write a song while on an airplane without the aid of a musical instrument because I can see AND hear where the notes go on a piece of manuscript paper. She challenged me, and I'm so glad she did.

After one semester of voice training, I felt there must be more for me to learn than what I was learning from my private voice instructor. Going to the Dean of Music at the end of that semester, I asked him if I could switch to another vocal studio. He told me of a new vocal instructor who would be joining the university as an artist-in-residence and that he needed to fill her studio. I was a bit skeptical, but he assured me that she, Dr. Jeri Graham-Edmonds, was a true master of all things vocal, and it just so happened that Dr. Graham-

Edmonds' own voice teacher would be conducting a recital that very night. He encouraged me to go because he told me she would be a great indication of what Dr. Graham-Edmonds would be like.

That very evening, I attended the vocal recital in which I was introduced to the voice of Madam Elena Nikolaidi. We were required to attend a certain number of recitals each semester, and I was in need of filling my quota anyway, so I thought, *What could it hurt?* When I discovered that Madam Nikolaidi was over seventy years old, I was incredulous, thinking to myself, *How good could this lady be?* And then she began to sing . . . with the voice of an angel, with the clarity and purity of an eighteen-year-old! I was enthralled and challenged, and I thought to myself, *If she sounds this amazing at seventy, she must be doing something right. I will learn from one of her students!* Thus began three and a half of the most difficult years of vocal training this world has ever known!

Dr. Jeri, as we called her, required that we record each thirty-minute vocal session in her studio and then review the techniques during the week using the tapes as a reference. She required us to learn the physical anatomy of the body that produces the voice. She required us to practice various breathing exercises daily. She required that we translate each word of our foreign language art songs into English so that we would understand what we were saying in order to better emote the song. But the most incredible thing she taught me? That the power of the voice is in the breath, and that the word for the Holy Spirit of God in Scripture is the same word in the Greek translated "breath." She taught me how to utilize my entire body as a conduit of the breath. She taught me the true power of singing lies within the power of God.

After one very stressful and confrontational vocal lesson, I remarked, "I am never going to sing an Italian aria or a French love song or a German folk song in church! How is this even relevant to what I want to do?" She gave me one of those Dr. Jeri gazes of steel, sat down at the piano, and began to sing a song of worship to the Lord. After a few seconds, it was obvious she did not even know I was there! After finishing the song, I was truly humbled. She continued the lesson with passion.

"You may not ever use an aria or operatic piece in worship, but the vocal techniques they help me relate to you are invaluable. There is no reason you cannot sing a pop song or a rock song or any type of song with excellent technique. There is no excuse for not using the best technique possible, young man. If you do as I say, you will sing until your dying day. If you do as I teach you, you can sing unhindered for hours upon hours. If you do as I say, I will help you learn how to talk correctly and even yell correctly so as to preserve your vocal instrument. Work hard for me, and I'll show you."

For the next four years, I worked my butt off for her. I knew I was not the most gifted singer. She had several students who could sing into the stratosphere with the greatest of ease and with such delicate control that it almost sounded surreal, so magical was their tone. But my greatest triumph came to me from Dr. Jeri on the last lesson I ever had with her. She began, "You do not have the greatest voice." The hesitation was about to become awkward when she continued. "But you are my best student. You've done everything I've asked you to do and then some. You will be singing when you're ninety years old." I melted, feeling overcome with such affirmation. Finally, my performance was paying off!

I must add this: I see Dr. Jeri from time to time and have had occasion to ask her about my technique. By the time that three and a half years in her studio ended, the techniques of breath control and body control and breath placement and stress reduction to free the voice had all become so second nature that I no longer even had to think about them; it's simply the way I sing. But I still want to make sure I'm singing with proper technique—that I haven't let anything slip. In 2011, I was invited to sing for Oklahoma Governor Mary Fallin's Inaugural Prayer gathering, and Dr. Jeri was the producer! After I sang, I asked Jeri, "How's my technique?" Her response? "You'll be singing when you're ninety."

As the cold winter chill of Oklahoma began to fill the air that first autumn at Oklahoma Baptist University, I realized I didn't have a winter coat, having worn out and outgrown the one I had used in high school. I called my folks and asked if they could help me buy a coat. They told me that cash was too short and that I'd have to put one in layaway and pay it out as I could. That same day, I went to the local Walmart and found the cheapest coat I could find and put it in layaway, putting only five dollars down to hold it there. This was embarrassing at times—having no coat in the winter, trying to make others think I simply had no need for a coat, that I was tough—not wanting them to think I was poor.

During this period of time, I couldn't afford gas for my car and had to walk to pretty much anywhere I couldn't bum a ride from a friend. The need for a coat and the need for gas forced me to seek out a job to supplement my non-existent income. The university food service had several openings, so I applied and got two jobs. Each morning, I served breakfast, and each evening, I served dinner. After serving breakfast and after serving dinner, I would go straight to the dish room and wash all the dishes that had just been used. At first I felt so belittled each time someone I knew would come through the line, but after a few weeks, my subservient existence grew bearable. . . mostly. It had not taken long for the jock crowd to single me out. An old familiar shock went through my entire being the first time I saw and heard one of the macho boys lean over to his buddy while glancing at me, "There's a fag." As I had learned in high school, I pretended I hadn't heard or seen anything, and I pretended everything was all right.

During that first semester, I had my first sexual encounter with another male while at OBU. Also in the music department, this young man and I had struck up a friendship. Both of us were in the B Theory class, and neither of us had any idea what was going on, so we had a lot in common. Spending more and more time together, we began to develop an emotional dependency between us. I'd never experienced feelings of jealousy over another male, but with him, I did. If he spent time with another male friend, I felt hurt. If he spoke to another male for too long, I felt threatened. And, as I look back now, he responded the same way to me.

One weekend, his roommate went home, and he invited me to spend the night in his room. As we talked, we began to tip-toe into the realm of things we'd experienced while in high school. He had been teased. He had been bullied. He had experimented with other boys sexually. One thing led to another and we found ourselves giving in to sexual experimentation of our own. As soon as the encounter ended, I felt so ashamed—partly because I had gone so long without an episode of sexual impurity and partly because I felt I had led him into sexual immorality. I immediately sought his forgiveness, telling him how I was now feeling, and he expressed similar feelings. I left his room without spending the night, so riddled was my mind with guilt and shame. Yet, these sexual encounters would come and go for the next three years.

In fact, over the coming four years at OBU, I would discover just how easy it was to be tempted with male-on-male sex and how many others felt trapped in the same way I felt. Our problem was that even though we felt shame and guilt after each encounter, we felt we had nowhere to turn for help. As it did in high school, the cycle of sexual failure and subsequent guilt and shame always led to more failure and even more guilt and shame. . . and grief. It felt as though we were in an ocean of all things God but with no lifeline TO Him. As in my younger years, the condemnation I felt from the "good church people" and their religious attitudes kept me from ever daring to share my burden with another person outside of my gay circle of friends.

But a glimmer of hope was on the way.

A GLIMMER OF HOPE

As I write this personal history, I realize that many who knew me during my college years—and even my years in grade and high school— may find it difficult to believe I experienced all that I did. But isn't that the nature of sin—to remain as hidden as possible? Not only did I want to keep the shameful nature of my sin from being discovered, but I had to keep the outward appearance of being a good boy from being uncovered to reveal the true weakness and frailty of my existence. It truly was an emotional juggling act. And I was a very good actor.

During my freshman year at OBU, I was introduced to several young men who struggled with same-sex attraction. With only one of those men did I experience sexual failure that year. Still in full performance mode, I would experience failure with this man and go right into penitence, punishing myself with shame and guilt and devising a performance agenda that might in some way help me find freedom—and more importantly, keep me from the perceived wrath of God that I felt He always directed my way. This became quite the cycle. Fail sexually, do good deeds. Fail sexually, pretend nothing had happened. Fail sexually, be so overcome with guilt and shame that I would determine to attend church more faithfully, to be kind to people, to do whatever I could do to serve. Pride and shame were a powerful tag team in my life. Pride kept me from seeking help. Shame kept me securely ensconced in the mire of future sexual failure.

During the next three years, I would encounter many young men who would approach me and, in my seasons of pride, I would rebuff them saying I wasn't gay. Nevertheless, those same young men would continue to pursue me, telling me they KNEW I was gay, they KNEW I wanted them, and they KNEW I would eventually give in, and whenever I do finally come to my senses, they would be there to help me accept my true identity. I knew they were right, but I had this one nagging problem: I just did not want to be gay!

Two of those young men grew to be dear friends of mine, but because I knew they struggled with issues the same as mine, I went out of my way to try and preserve the friendships—meaning I never allowed myself to get into compromising sexual situations with them. My perception was that homosexual relations were for pleasure, pure and simple, and I did not want my friends to feel used—ever.

During our sophomore year, one of these friends went into an emotional spiral—had a mental breakdown—from simply trying to not be gay. In an effort to console him, I went to his room and told him that I also struggled with my sexual identity but that I considered it an anomaly—that it was indeed abnormal but something I thought could be fixed. In fact, I told him of a young man on campus who had been cured. Rumor was that this certain man, being from a very wealthy family, had received professional counseling for the disorder, and it had been successful. I had no idea if the rumor was true, but it sounded good to me. The friend I was trying to encourage didn't believe me. And, if I'm to be honest, I didn't really believe it at the time either.

During this time, I occasionally dated women, hoping to be seen as straight and hoping that these dates would somehow fix me. Another friend would double-date with me and my date. Both of us were under the assumption that if we could be around women enough, our desires would begin to transform. We both failed horribly (more on that later), he going headlong into the gay lifestyle, fully embracing homosexuality as his identity. When he contracted AIDS a few years after our college graduation, he called and asked me if I would sing at his funeral. I assured him that I would be glad to but that I would not hesitate to tell about my own freedom should the subject come up (I know, I'm jumping ahead a bit). He told me that would be fine with him. Upon his death, I received word from his family that there would be men stationed at the door to the church to keep me from entering so as to not bring disrespect to a life and a sexual identity the family had come to embrace. Mortified and wounded, I sadly did not go to the funeral. This would not be the only time this would occur in my life. Back to my story.

One man was so adamant and such a pursuer that he would just "happen" to be in the showers when I was there. Being in the habit of trying to shower when no one else was there, he caught on to my routine and would be standing there whenever I stepped out of the shower. On one occasion, he grabbed my penis. I recoiled in disgust and horror, telling him to never do that again. All he said? "You know you liked it. I can see it in your eyes." As weird as it seems, although I was genuinely taken aback by his inappropriate touch, I felt something I longed for. I felt *wanted*.

After several similar encounters over the next few weeks, I felt I had gained sufficient power over these come-ons that I began to let my guard down, just pretending these advances didn't bother me at all and were no big deal to rebuff. We actually began to develop a sort of friendship. I knew he was often teased by the jocks on campus as being gay, so I sort of felt a need to be his friend, to just make him feel valuable. On one particular weekend, he noticed I was feeling lonely, most of my other friends having gone for the weekend and me having to stay and work. He simply said, "Come spend the night in my room. My roommate's gone for the weekend. We can just talk."

As we prepared for bed, he stripped down into nothing, announcing to me that he slept in the nude. From there we began to talk about all manner of things from personal feelings about God to deep hidden things we had not shared with anyone else. As our conversation grew more and more sexual in nature, he began to make sexually suggestive overtones, finally simply asking me if I wanted to have sex with him. I still would not allow him to touch me, yet I felt like a complete and utter failure for even allowing myself to be in such a position. I was filled with shame immediately and waited for him to fall asleep so I could sneak from the room and wallow in my shame in my own room—alone. What a life.

Temptation. Lust. Failure. Shame. Guilt. Regret. Penance. Performing for God's approval once again. Walking in my own strength once again. Feeling good about myself if my performance was at a high enough level (whatever *that* is!). Temptation. Repeat cycle over and over and over again. During the next few years, I still told myself I was not gay, that somehow I would get "fixed"—pretty much walking in complete denial. Funny, but living by one's performance always tends to lead to destruction, and I was well on my way. It would be several years before I was to discover the secret to ending the performance games and learning the value of real relationships, real love, real intimacy as ordained by God, and real freedom from same-sex attraction.

Even though I felt hopeless and alone most of the time, I can look back and see precious glimpses of God's hand in my life, even in college. During my freshman year, I was introduced to contemporary Christian music. Until that time, the most contemporary Christian music I had heard was the southern Gospel music we watched on TV every Sunday morning on a show called the *Gospel Singing Jubilee* which featured popular artists like the Florida Boys, the Speers, and the Happy Goodman Family. I also remember hearing Grandpa Jones sing southern Gospel on a popular country variety show of the day called *Hee Haw*. Of course, I also had a hymns album by none other than Elvis Presley. That was the extent of what I considered contemporary Christian music from the time I was a boy, but that all changed.

A fellow freshman, a friend from Albuquerque, New Mexico, handed me a recording by a popular Christian rock band called *2nd Chapter of Acts*. As she handed me the record, I was drawn to the scraggly looking trio on the cover. "Hippie music?" I asked in exasperation. "You want me to listen to *hippie* music?"

She went on to tell me how this band had helped usher in the Jesus Movement. I had never heard of such a thing! As she went on, I was amazed that I could've missed so much history in the making, but it also shows how far back in the woods I had lived while growing up. The Jesus Movement was a spiritual revival that began in southern California among the youth of the hippie culture in the late 1960s and rapidly spread throughout the nation during the 1970s and coming to a close in the 1980s. I'd missed most of it.

Now intrigued, I listened to the music of *2nd Chapter of Acts*—Annie Herring and her siblings, Matthew and Nellie Ward. As I heard their amazing familial harmonies, I was mesmerized. As I listened to the words, I was challenged and convicted that I didn't know God like these people seemed to know Him. And the more I got to know about the lives of this musical family, the more I discovered that maybe, just maybe, there was hope for me. Why did I believe that?

Somehow I heard Annie (Ward) Herring's story. Good Catholic girl from North Dakota. Went to LA to make it in the music business. Signed by a major record label to be the next Janis Joplin. Delving into the sex, drugs, and the rock-and-roll life of the music scene, Annie Ward became pregnant. Twice. Gave those babies up for adoption. She meets big-time producer, Buck Herring. They wed and were soon born again. Their lives had been revolutionized by God's redeeming love. Within two years of one another, Annie's parents passed away, leaving her little sister and brother, Nellie and Matthew, in need of a home. God sent them to live with big sister and her husband.

As Annie sought to know the Lord, and as she learned to receive His love, songs began to pour out of her. Not knowing how to play the piano, she simply trusted Jesus to show her where to place her hands, and this amazing flood of songs began to pour out of her life. Along with Nellie and Matthew, the trio began to sing in coffee shops around town, and before you know it, they had a recording contract with a secular label.

On their very first recording, called *With Footnotes*, was a song called *He Loves Me*. The lyrics of that song began to haunt my mind in a good way. Singing and screaming by the end of the song, "He took away my sin and shame! He took away my sin and shame! He loves me! He loves me! He loves me! Hallelujah!," I was at once drawn to the music and the possibility of God loving me like He loved Annie, yet I was discouraged by my own self-evaluation that there was no way God could love me.

Never had I heard such lyrics. At first I was incredulous that since these songs were not from the hymnal they must somehow be sacrilegious. How's that for self-righteous indignation and plain old stupidity? At times I would be so angry at what was being sung simply because I could not believe God could love me like He seemed to love those singers, and at times I allowed my need to perform for approval to permeate and cloud my perception. They seemed to trash the idea of even needing to perform at all—that somehow and in some way, God just loved them because of who they were!

They messed with my head. Messed me up to the point of countless tears amid countless listening sessions, at times playing the entire record back to back to back to back, at times playing one song over and over and over again, getting up from the floor and wiping away the tears and dropping the needle on the groove of the record to start the needed song anew (ask your parents or grandparents about dropping the needle). This went on for four years, from my freshman year until my senior year, and even beyond. But there was someone else God wanted me to listen to— another musician who would challenge me and keep me seeking Him, even when I felt He was unreachable.

UNREACHABLE

Being so new to the world of contemporary Christian music, I'd never heard of most of the popular artists of the day—the groundbreakers, the legends. In the late '70s and early '80s, I was introduced to the music of LoveSong, Dallas Holm, Andrae Crouch and the Disciples, Larry Norman, Resurrection Band, Phil Keaggy, Michael and Stormie Omartian, Nancy Honeytree, Reba Rambo, and Evie Tornquist, and I felt like I'd died and gone to heaven musically! It was as if all my wildest dreams had come true. Here were amazing musicians and songwriters singing songs that were born out of their own lives that were relevant, relatable! I was so accustomed to and programmed to revere the hymns of the church that I found it difficult to give myself permission to love this music! While I still dearly love the old hymns of the faith, I found few songs that related to my personal struggles. The music of Annie Herring and *2nd Chapter of Acts* was the first, but then came another.

I believe it was in the spring of 1978 when I first heard the name, Keith Green. Another friend in my theory class showed me a record album by this man, who looked like a wild man with his curly 'fro and full beard. This friend told me Keith would be on our campus in concert that very night and that he thought I would love his music and message. When I arrived at the concert, there were only about 200 students there. My personal thought was, *How good could this guy be if only a handful of students are willing to show up?* Man, was I ever in for a shock!

As he walked out to the piano, no band on stage, I thought he looked so non-celebrity, as if he were going out of his way to look normal, to not draw attention to himself. My reaction upon seeing him, for some odd reason, was that he looked like I imagined John the Baptist must've looked. And then Keith began to speak, and I thought to myself, *Yep, that's John the Baptist alright,* so fiery in his manner of delivery, so full of passion. As he spoke, he was very bold in his beliefs. He seemed so adamant that everyone in attendance come to know Jesus—to REALLY come to know Him, not just take His name. I felt so convicted that he somehow knew I was hiding, playing games. But then Keith began to sing, and I was undone.

"I was lost in a fantasy that blinded me until Your love broke through..." Never had I heard someone sing a song so passionately. It was like hearing the Annie Herring song, *He Loves Me,* for the first time. This guy really believes God loves him. As the evening wore on, it was as if Keith forgot we were even there, so intimate was his musical conversation with God. Like listening in on a private conversation between two best friends, I was uncomfortable at first with such stark and unashamed intimacy. I wondered if I should even be listening. But the effect was just as stark and just as real. The awareness in every part of my being that God was there in our midst was unavoidable, like the weight of His presence was so real I could've cut the air with a knife. I was reduced to fear and trembling and feelings of being loved.

As the enemy would have it, he soon did a number on my own mind. Thoughts like, *That song is for Keith, not for you, Dennis. You are unworthy of singing such a song to such a holy God* and *What a hypocrite you are, pretending that God could possibly love you when everyone around you in this room knows the truth. They're just too kind to tell you how pitiful they think you are.* Thinking such thoughts after brief face-to-face encounters with God always shattered any hope I'd managed to feel.

For the next few years, along with the music of Annie Herring, God would use this man's music to keep me from taking my own life.

Going about my life of performance left me so empty inside. In those days, I would latch on to anyone who showed me any bit of attention. Sometimes that worked out for the better—most of the time, not so much. But in my need to perform in order to be accepted by others, I would play the religious games of the day, pretending right along with whatever the religious crowd deemed spiritual. There was a group on campus called the Baptist Student Union (now called Baptist Collegiate Ministries), headed by a man named Bob Burgess. I had heard there was a discipleship program offered by the BSU and had heard many stories of how God was transforming the lives of fellow students through it. My first reaction upon being invited to attend a BSU meeting was the thought, *I don't want to be anywhere near such spiritual snobs.* I felt that everyone in the BSU looked down on me. That was a lie, but I believed it, nonetheless.

Reluctantly, I decided to attend one night. Mainly desperation led me there. As Bob spoke, I felt great love and compassion coming from him. Waiting around afterward to talk with him, I almost walked out because so many students clamored for his attention, so as usual I allowed the voice of the enemy to sway me. *He doesn't have time for you. See how he fawns over the lovable students? You are an abject loser. Why would he even know or care that you exist?* As I turned to walk out, a voice called out to me from somewhere in the crowd.

"Hey, Dennis. Wait a minute!"

Turning around to see who had spoken, Bob emerged from the group and was headed directly for me! I felt as if I would melt and burst into tears right on the spot. Bob immediately welcomed me and thanked me for attending, and as only Bob could do, he went straight to the heart of the matter. "Why did you come, Dennis?"

"A friend invited me," I responded.

"No. That's not what I mean. Why are you here? What do you need? What were your expectations?"

Feeling painted into a corner with nowhere to run, I responded with a stutter, "I...I...uh...er...I want to be discipled. I want to be more like Jesus." Of course, this was simply the most religious "act" I could put on to make him like me, to let me in. I think Bob saw right through me, but he played along.

"If you're serious, I'll assign you a discipleship buddy and give you our discipleship study book. You'll be required to come each week with your lesson studied and be willing to be held accountable in all areas of your life. We don't want to control you; we just want to help you begin to think about the lies you're believing and help you learn to put them off and to put on the truth."

Like a joke going right over a naive person's head, Bob's words meant very little to me in that moment. My expectations were to be told how good I was, to be showered with praise, to be accepted by the religious elite as I saw them, to be loved. Of course, I washed right out of the course because my mind could not take adding one more layer to the heavy load of performances I was already in the middle of. I would avoid Bob for the rest of my OBU days, and that wasn't easy.

Four days a week, the BSU sponsored a worship gathering called Noon Days in a small campus chapel. For thirty minutes the students would pack out the little structure, sitting shoulder to shoulder and all the aisles filled with standing-room-only overflow most days, and they would simply sing songs of worship to God. Bob usually sat somewhere up front, so I could easily avoid him if I were able to sneak in the back of the room. Though I didn't know why at the time, I would sit there as the singing began and, before I knew it, the feelings of loneliness and depression and despair would leave me. And whenever I felt confident enough to join in with the singing, the feelings were elevated to even greater heights. Joy! Ecstasy! Peace. Love.

Each time I went, I left feeling victorious. But these feelings dissipated far too quickly whenever the reality of my life came back into focus. It was as if, for a few brief moments, I had reached for and actually found whatever it was I'd been searching for. But just as quickly, those feelings were always replaced with the utter and abject reality that I was so far away from the hope of that feeling that I was actually unreachable. Hopeless was my middle name. And, of course, this juxtaposition of darkness and light sent me reeling right back into the downward spiral from whatever lofty height I'd tricked myself into believing I had actually reached. Though I know it now, I couldn't see that such moments of peace and joy and assurance, no matter how brief, were actually the hand of God trying to reach into my life and rescue me. What a fool I was in those days.

There were other little glimpses of God trying to reach into my life. During my sophomore year, I mentioned to one of the girls in my choir that I'd never had a surprise birthday party and how much something like that would mean to me. Not thinking anything about it, I went about business as usual. Then one night, not long after that brief statement to my friend, she called and asked me to come to her dorm to help her with something. As I walked into the front entrance, I expected to see her there waiting for me. After a few minutes, she came in from the parlor area and asked me to follow her. No sooner had we entered the darkened room than the lights suddenly turned on, and a chorus of people began to shout, "Happy birthday!" Bursting into song, this wonderful chorus of love so overwhelmed me that I began to sob…and sob…and sob…

And then they began to shower me with gifts! When one feels as unlovable as I felt in those days, the emotional tank becomes so impacted that with the slightest of emotional tugs, all that pent-up emotion comes pouring out. That's exactly what happened to me. For the next hour, I felt love like I'd not felt in a long time come over me. Like a prince in the king's court, I felt so honored and wanted and worth something…and loved. And then, they loaded me up in a car and drove me around town, laughing and simply driving around for the sheer joy of being together. As with those Noon Day gatherings, I felt a glorious respite from the normal pressure to perform for acceptance. But just as with Noon Day, the feelings were dashed to bits whenever the party was over and I had to walk back to my dorm room...alone.

I remember feeling so defeated and wondering if those wondrous feelings I'd just experienced could ever be a constant reality in my life. Like a lost man wandering hopelessly around in a desert, I was constantly teased with the mirage of an oasis of love and acceptance and joy and peace, only to dive into the middle of the pool and come up with a mouthful of sand and bitterness. But not to worry—my feelings of worthlessness would be validated soon enough, and I would truly understand the feeling of being unreachable...without hope.

DATING FOR THE CURE

It was during my first day of music theory class my sophomore year when my life was changed forever, but I wouldn't have a clue as to the extent of that change for several years. She sashayed into the room and sat right on the front row. I, of course, sat on the back row in the hope that I would never be called on to answer a question.

Melinda Hewitt was absolutely stunning, and she seemed to know it. With dark brown hair cascading around her perfect face, her blue eyes sent shock waves through my system and left me staring at those amazing lips that reminded me of one of my favorite actresses, Bernadette Peters. I was enthralled with Melinda's stunning beauty but felt not one iota of sexual attraction to her. While the other guys seemed to fall all over themselves to get to her, I sat shyly in my seat and pretended I was as aroused by her as they seemed to be. It's one thing to appreciate great beauty, yet quite another to try to feel any sexual draw to that beauty when none is there. And that's where I sat squarely for those first few weeks.

Often, as I sat there staring at her, I'd imagine myself being married to her. I could see us raising the nine children I'd imagined I'd have one day (that was a thought I'd carried since I was a boy— that I'd one day be dad to nine kids. See how insane I'd become?). Of course, I felt that if I were ever able to ask her out and be romantic with her, she'd never say yes because she was so far out of my league. But the more I thought about it, the more I began to ponder a way to fix myself. If I could ever date a girl so physically beautiful, then perhaps just being around her enough would begin to change my way of thinking, and sexual arousal WOULD one day come as the result of my thoughts toward a person of the opposite sex.

Confiding in one of my male friends who was just as gay as I was, he encouraged me to ask her out, agreeing with me that it couldn't hurt and just might help! It just so happened that a group of us were planning a trip to Six Flags over Texas. Knowing she was from Dallas herself, I assumed that Melinda would be more inclined to go with me since it was an area she was very familiar with. And she might want to go with me just to get a free trip back home, even if it did involve a worthless, scrawny country bumpkin like me!

So I got up my nerve and approached her after class. "A few of us are going to Six Flags this weekend. Would you like to go with me?"

She looked at me with great sympathy. I braced myself for the big letdown. "I'm so sorry, but I already have a commitment for this weekend and can't go, but I'd really like to. Ask me again sometime."

All I heard was, "Sorry, but no," having developed the most useful trait of hearing one thing but concocting and believing another. It took several months before I would ask her out again. Little did I know, but Melinda honestly did have something else she couldn't get out of. And of even greater surprise was the fact that she honestly HAD wanted to go with me, that she DID find me attractive, and that she DID like me "like that"!

As she and her friends would have it, they began devising a plan to get me to ask her out again. So naïve was I to the ways and wiles of a woman that it did not dawn on me how often Melinda would just happen to be standing right outside the door to my psychology class, even though she didn't have a class in that building. It never once occurred to me that she would, by sheer coincidence, be practicing her piano piece in the room next to mine in Ford Music Hall and pop in the door to my practice room just to say hello. And then, the piece de resistance: I came out of Ford Music Hall to find every window of my Galaxie 500 covered with bright red lipstick imprints of Melinda's lips—those wonderful Bernadette Peters-esque lips!

Not knowing what to do, I thought of walking away and pretending not to know whose car it was, but then a couple of my buddies noticed and began to chide me. "Who did this? Who likes you, man? Tell us!" I could feel my face growing red as the embarrassment took control. Of course, I immediately knew who it was. I told them Melinda had done it, and they acted like that was the most impossible thing in the world to believe—that someone like HER would even consider going out with someone like ME! I honestly had to agree, but was, at the same time, intrigued.

Not having the slightest clue as to how to approach her again since it had been so long since the first time I asked her out, I confessed to one of Melinda's roommates, Judy, that I didn't even know HOW to ask her out. But I needed not fear; Judy had been in on the scheme from the beginning, and I had just stepped squarely into the very elaborate trap and plan they had prepared for me.

Without missing a beat, Judy went right into the script with an Oscar-worthy performance. "Dennis, she's running on the track tonight about six o'clock, and I'm a bit concerned with her safety. I think you could impress her by simply offering to run with her or to watch out for her while she runs. Just show up at the track, and I bet she'll love the company."

With surgeon-like precision, the plan worked perfectly (their plan, that is!). I showed up at the track and watched for her to run around to the side where I waited for her. Once there, I simply said, "Are you running alone?" to which she replied, "Yes, but I'm fine."

The chivalry kicked in as I found myself saying, "I'd feel more comfortable about you being here if you weren't alone. Would you mind if I ran with you?"

"No, of course not. I'd actually love the company."

Not once did it occur to me that she had used the exact same phrase Judy had used to get me there—"love the company." As we ended our run, we began to talk, and as we talked, she asked me why I had not asked her out again. After explaining to her how it had felt to be rejected, she went on to tell me that she really couldn't have gone but that she honestly had wanted to go with me. With that, I did the bravest thing I recall ever having done to that point. I took her by the hand, leaned into her beautiful face, and kissed her.

That same year, we decided to sing a song together for the school talent show. As we approached one another from opposite sides of the stage, we sang the song *Suddenly* from the Olivia Newton-John movie, *Xanadu*. "Suddenly, the wheels are in motion, and I, I, I, I am suddenly filled with emotion." In that moment, I felt an emotional connection to her that would endure for the next three years, even though that emotion never tipped the scale toward sexual arousal for me. It continued to give me a sort of hope that if I continued to fake it, I'd eventually make it. We dated off and on for the rest of that year. And off and on for our junior year. And off and on for our senior year. The break-ups always came when I felt the most pressure. Before any banquet or awards ceremony or gathering in which a date was expected, I would bolt because in my mind that meant we were getting serious, and I saw no way to surrender to a serious relationship in which I had no hope of finding sexual fulfillment. On top of that was the pressure I felt with the realization that I would never be able to satisfy her physical needs.

Our final breakup was absolutely heartbreaking. The way in which I carried it out was mean and cruel and wrong, but I felt I had to make this one who so obviously loved me come to a place of utter hatred of me. Why? So she could forget about me and move on to a better life than one she could ever possibly have with me. What tipped me right over the edge emotionally had nothing to do with Melinda. Beside Jesus, she's the best thing that's ever happened to me. That she is still with me to this day is nothing short of a miracle from my point of view.

As much as I had wanted Melinda to be my cure, she was not. She could not be. While with her, I felt hopeful, but with one act of betrayal on the part of one I trusted most, my world and all thoughts of hope came crashing down into utter ruin and devastation.

THE NIGHT THAT CHANGED EVERYTHING

Throughout the four years of my college career, I had moments of abstinence, not freedom. The fear of being found out kept me from being more promiscuous than I was. More than once I heard fellow students say things under their breath about me. I'd catch them eyeing me and whispering to a friend, "He's a fag" or "There's that fag I was telling you about." I pretended to not notice, but they wanted me to notice. One summer I shared an apartment with some buddies. While I was at the pool at the apartment, I heard several of the jocks around the pool snickering and pointing at me. "Why are all the faggots at the pool every day?" said one guy, loud enough for me to hear. "This is where they come to check out each other's butts!" responded the other. "Too many queers around here."

It was moments like these that not only sent me back to remembrances of my earlier days in high school but also served to send me into an ever-deepening and out-of-control spiral into hopelessness. My reasoning? If everyone else could see that in me—see what I felt about myself—then it must be true. There is no way out. There is no hope. In moments like these, I simply pretended to not hear and would find some excuse to go back and hide out in my apartment.

As the summer came to a close and my senior year of college got underway, an ever-increasing feeling that I'd been able to suppress for most of my college days began to bubble uncontrollably to the surface. I knew that school would soon be over, and God had not met me here. For years I had begged Him to change me, and nothing had changed; it had only gotten worse. What would I do once college is over? How would I ever be able to face the realities of the world—more specifically, my homosexuality—with any semblance of sanity? I felt as though the world was closing in on me, and that soon enough everyone would know everything about me. I would not be able to maintain my charade forever. This was when thoughts of suicide first became real in my life.

I was a desperate man. As I'd always done, I kept a sliver of hope alive. There were still a few months of school left before graduation. Perhaps God might yet intervene and set me free from the bondage of homosexuality. I begged God to change me. Night after night as I lay in bed, I pondered what that change might look like. I remember feeling more hopeless than ever, wondering if anyone would dare to take an interest in my life, to take an interest in me—not for what I could do for them but for simply being ME.

I felt utterly worthless. I considered myself lower than a worm that crawls in the dirt. But those thoughts were shattered the day I heard my name called. Turning around to see who had spoken, I was shocked to realize that someone like him was daring to talk to someone like me. I, the worm, was being addressed by a Christian leader in our community—husband, father, religious fixture, a well-respected citizen known by everyone. At first I thought he must've called for someone else—that I had heard incorrectly—but then he called my name again.

"How are you doing, young man?" he asked. To myself I was thinking, "How do you even know who I am?" But I replied shyly, "I'm fine."

"How are your studies going? I've been impressed by your performances in Glee Club."

"Thank you, sir."

"I'd like to get to know you. One of the callings of my life is to come alongside young men like yourself and to help you out if I can. If nothing else, I can pray for you, or at least be a sympathetic shoulder to lean on, as you prepare to graduate."

I was shocked yet felt so valued. And as the days went by, he made good on what he had said. Each week, he'd call me and ask how my studies were going. He'd ask if I had any burdens he could pray with me about. At other times, he'd sense that I was being overwhelmed by a paper or by preparation for a test, so he would swing by the dorm, pick me up, and take me out for a Coke. His love for movies was also inspiring to me because movies were a wonderful escape for my weary soul. He'd take me to see movies, and he would pay for *everything!* Talk about feeling loved and valued and worthwhile! What I didn't realize was that he was making a great investment in my life, and I was feeling more and more free every day. Funny, but love has a way of setting a heart free, doesn't it?

When the fall semester of my senior year began, I decided to not live in the dorm but to get an apartment so I could be alone and as far away as possible from temptation and what I perceived others thought of me. Near the end of that semester, while in my apartment, a fellow student whom I suspected was also struggling with same-sex attraction, dropped by to see me. He sat on my bed while I reclined. After a few minutes of small talk, he inched closer and closer to my side of the bed, and before I knew it, he had placed his hand on my thigh. This sent me into panic mode. I'd been doing so well, and now *this!* I cut him off and pretended nothing had happened and simply told him I'd forgotten I was supposed to meet someone in the University Center. As I quickly ushered him out of the apartment, I was once again assailed with thoughts of raging homosexuality. As if a crushing weight had been placed upon my mind, I felt as hopeless as ever in that moment. But at least now I had someone I could turn to. My friend could help me; I just had a feeling.

In my panic, I called him and told him, "I need to talk."

"What is it?" he asked.

Trembling with fear and despair, I said, "There's something I'm hiding. Been hiding for a long time. I'm scared to death to tell you or anyone else what it is. I'm so ashamed. I need help. I really need help."

After I hung up the phone, I went outside and waited for him to pick me up. As his car came to a stop, I felt such relief. Knowing someone thought enough of me to come for me, I already felt rescued! As I sat down, he began to drive. I asked him where we could talk privately. He told me he had a friend with an apartment and that the friend was not at home that week—that he had been watching the place for him. We could talk there, and not one soul would hear us. He assured me that I would be safe there. It felt so good to have someone simply understand my need to feel protected and cared for in the manner in which this man I'd grown to respect so much demonstrated to me. Panic had begun to lift and trust was taking its place.

As we entered the apartment, he told me to sit. He sat in a chair directly in front of me where he could make direct eye contact with me. Feeling so ashamed, I could not bear the thought of letting this man down with what I was about to tell him. He was so patient with me, so caring. My fear began to subside simply because of his willingness to wait for my readiness. Peace.

"What is it, son? he asked after he felt I was ready.

I began with great hesitation. Even though I had shared my secret with other men by being sexually active with them, this was different. This was someone who was not tainted by same-sex attraction. This was someone I trusted and respected, and, ultimately, someone I sensed could help me.

"I'm dying on the inside," I began. "I've been hiding something my entire life, and it's crushing me. I feel like my head's going to explode most of the time. I just can't help myself. I don't know what to do, and I'm scared to death of how you'll respond."

Touching my hand, he said, "Son, there's nothing you can share with me that I've not heard before. There's nothing you can share with me that could possibly keep me from loving you. You can trust me . . . when you're ready. Just take your time."

As if ice water was running through my veins, I began to shake. It felt like I was going to pass out, and I remember thinking that in that moment, losing consciousness actually sounded like a good thing. As I sat there for a couple more minutes, he again took my hand and began to squeeze it, saying, "Just tell me. It'll be okay."

In that moment, I felt a rush of trust well up in me. Turning my face upward for the first time in this awkward conversation, I looked him in the eye and said, "I think I'm homosexual. And I don't know what to do. Can you help me?"

He calmly looked me right in the eye and said, "I completely understand."

That one phrase—I completely understand—sent waves of relief through my mind. I felt the coldness dissipate and a warmth of hope replace the coldness in my body. I stopped shaking and felt utter peace. It was as if the entire weight of the world had suddenly been lifted from my shoulders. And then it happened.

"I really do understand," he went on. "More than you know."

Taking me by the hand, he pulled me up from the chair, led me into the bedroom, and had me lie down on the bed. He began to tell me how he had those same feelings for me, and he began to unzip my pants.

I gave up.

After the encounter, I was silent. As if my mind had become numb to what had just happened, emotion died in me that night. Words that should've been said couldn't even be formed due to the searing pain in my mind in that moment. I know now that I was in shock. I remember feeling as if I weren't even present in the room when the encounter was taking place—as if I was somewhere above, watching something happen that should not be happening, yet I WAS there. And I had nothing left. Nothing.

As he drove me back to my apartment, he tried to make conversation with me. "You realize this is normal for you and me." I couldn't believe he could talk; I couldn't speak. "This is just another way God made us to love, and this *is* love, son."

Son. He kept calling me son.

As he came to a stop in front of my apartment, he took my hand in both of his and squeezed it and began to pray. I thought I would throw up. After he said his amens, he asked, "When can I see you again?" I simply got out of the car and never spoke with him again. The damage had been done.

As if caught in a whirlwind with no way of calming the storm, my mind swirled with guilt and shame and thoughts. I felt betrayed. I felt used. I had committed adultery . . . with a *man!* Rushing up the stairs and into my apartment, I locked the door, turned on the gas heater, and did not light the flame. I couldn't do this anymore. I could not go on. I was done.

Some of the craziest thoughts began reeling in my head. My parents will be better off without me. My brothers won't have to be ashamed of their fag of a brother. The world will be a better place without me. And on and on. Now that I look back and recall thinking such thoughts, it's easy to see just how self-centered and self-focused I had become—like I could possibly know what was best for my parents or my brothers! Like I knew more and better than God about my life! As I lay there, a weird sort of peace came over me. I would not have to struggle much longer, and that felt wonderful.

After a couple of minutes, I had become used to the smell of the gas, but then one thought began to override all the other thoughts crowding my mind: "Are you ready for eternity? Do you know what waits for you out there? Are you really ready to die?" I couldn't answer those questions with a yes. And I began to panic again—so much so that I got up from the floor and quickly shut off the gas. Sitting back down on the floor, I simply made this statement to myself. "This is just the way I was born. Stop fighting it, man. Just *be* who you were born to be, and peace will come."

And peace did come.

REMEMBER MELINDA

As the fall semester of 1980 ended, I was more confused than ever yet strangely at peace, simply by coming to the conclusion that same-sex attraction was my lot in life. I still had moments of thinking I could fix myself if I just tried harder, so I continued to see Melinda off and on—but mostly off. We dated during my senior year, and even had some moments when I kissed her, but I continued to feel like I could never perform if it came down to having sex with her. But more than that, I honestly didn't want her to feel as used as I felt after I had sex with other men. As was my practice—and I never saw this until years later—when it came time for the fall Thanksgiving banquets or the Christmas banquets common at our school, I would break things off with Melinda.

In my mind, going to a banquet meant a very public presentation of a couple, and I felt utterly incapable of handling the pressure to perform. Public displays of affection were not the norm for me yet were expected by Melinda. The most I could muster up was to hold her hand, and even then I felt tremendous pressure to perform. You see, in my mind I was still thinking people would look at me with a woman and say to themselves "What a fake! That queer is trying to pretend he's straight!" I was honestly my own worst enemy!

That Christmas, I once again broke up with Melinda, sending her off with a broken heart for Christmas. The guilt and shame of my hidden sin, coupled with the realization that I'd deeply wounded someone so precious, was like a double-edged sword slicing through my mind. My downward spiral began with that breakup and continued to plummet when I went back to the little apartment I called home. Alone. Again. Forever.

Christmas was not fun for me that year, and I LOVE Christmas! I love everything about it. The story of Jesus and the carols. Seeing relatives and opening gifts. Turkey and pumpkin pie. The sights, the sounds, the smells. And most of all, the FEELINGS surrounding Christmas. But with the weight of the guilt and shame I had, there was not much of anything even faintly resembling joy. "Have yourself a miserable little Christmas" would have been the lyric I sang!

All during my senior year, I worked at a Chinese restaurant called Mandarin Garden, a five-star eating establishment where the waiters all wore tuxes and spun plates in a flamboyant display meant to wow the revelers. At first I worked as a busboy but then was promoted to waiter. From that point on, during the week I waited tables and on Friday nights, I played the restaurant piano, providing pleasant sounds for the diners. Being paid only by tips, happy diners would deposit in the brandy snifter placed on the piano. I learned very quickly to play the songs people requested. Having been given several fake books by my Aunt Gladys, I could whip out any of the standard pop catalog from the 1920s all the way to the modern 1980s.

As soon as the new year came, and before school was back in session, I went back to my little apartment so I could go back to work at Mandarin Garden. For the month of January, I went to work almost every day and then came back to the emptiness of my room. I had to walk up those dreary steps; had to listen to the little newlywed couple making love in the apartment next door night after night; had to turn on the gas heating stove and light the flame, still contemplating whether I'd made the right decision by not taking my life; had to walk across that floor where only a few weeks before I had laid down to die. To say my life was depressing would be an understatement.

The week before school was to be back in session, I once again felt I would lose my mind due to the mental battles I faced just to survive. Such was my longing to know and to be known by another human being that I began to build very unhealthy emotional attachments to other guys. Not sexual attractions per se, but real heavy-duty emotional dependencies. This usually resulted in my actually driving away the very ones I wanted in my life. In fact, during my junior year of college, I was in a quartet called The Fallen Angels (How appropriate was that?) with three seniors. Being so close to those guys due to our heavy rehearsal schedule and frequent concerts made them a very natural focus for me.

I needed their affirmation so much that I'd just show up wherever they were. If I couldn't find one, I'd immediately go in search of one of another and just attach myself to whatever he was doing. My hope was that they would not catch on to just how needy I was. My longing was that they would see me as one of them, meaning I wanted them to see me as I perceived others saw *them*—well-respected, manly men. From my perspective, I saw myself as a mere boy among men. I saw them as having it all together and me being an emotional basket case. All I could see was how much I lacked when compared to them. By the end of my junior year, I had convinced myself that they truly were the answer to my problems. But something always happened to bring me right back down.

During my senior year, I longed so to hear from any of my old quartet buddies who had graduated and had gone on to graduate school. I took it so hard when, week after expectant week, I heard nothing from any of them. Of course I felt unloved and forgotten. Worthless. Reality was that they had gone on with their lives, and reality was that real life and time and distance naturally and normally have a way of leaving even once-close friends distant. It didn't mean they didn't love me. But my mind told me otherwise.

As I said before, as the week before the spring semester was to begin, *all* the weight of *all* the loss, and *all* the burden of *all* the pain and depression had left me in sheer panic mode. I had no one I could truly call friend—not because of them but because I could never allow myself to get too emotionally close to the ones who truly cared for me lest they discover my secret and reject me. So imagine my constant battle—so emotionally needy that I'd cling to those I considered strong and masculine to the point that I'd drive them away, all while never allowing myself to get honestly and intimately close to anyone. For all intents and purposes, I had driven myself to the edge of a cliff overlooking a dark abyss of hopelessness.

For some reason, that feeling of hopelessness led me to do one of the wisest things I ever did in my college career. I moved out of my apartment and back into a private room in the men's dorm, telling myself that even if I could never truly be close to anyone, I should at least be around other people. Though it was still not very healthy—living alone yet surrounded by others—it was better than living alone with no one around.

It was during that spring semester that I, in one of my needy episodes, latched on to another man on my floor. I'll call him Jim. Jim simply made the mistake of paying attention to me. I soon found myself looking for him everywhere I went. If I thought he was at the practice hall, I'd find an excuse to just happen to be in the practice room next to his. Finding out when he took his meals in the cafeteria, I found myself coincidentally showing up with my meal tray at his table. If he was playing ping-pong in the recreation room, so was I. If I heard he was going to be at a certain campus event, I made sure and found my way to where he was. In addition to my frequent planned encounters, I would often draw pictures and give him gifts, expecting my lavish generosity to buy me perhaps a bit more of his affection.

And then the most amazing thing began to happen.

Jim began to welcome my intrusions, even making me feel that he actually enjoyed my presence! Though I never could convince myself that he was actually concerned for me (that pesky feeling of worthlessness), I found glimmers of life simply by being in a relationship with another human being . . . no matter how dysfunctional it was in actuality. Talk about ramping up my pursuit! I became ultra-clingy. Sickeningly clingy. As I look back, it's easy to see just how far I had sunken in my utter depravity. It was as if I was groveling in the vile refuse of a swine's muddy pen.

As was usually the case, I somehow talked myself back into seeing if I could date Melinda one more time, just on the outside chance that maybe now, since I was feeling a bit better about myself, heterosexuality would kick in. Dating once again placed a lot of pressure on me, and once again, mid-semester, I broke things off with her. Once again, she left shattered. If it had been me, I would've written off the relationship a long time ago.

Near the end of that semester came my required senior recital presentation. This recital represented my final project and was to be a huge part of my grade. As the night to make my presentation came, I was more nervous than ever, feeling the pressure to make my parents proud, feeling the need to impress my vocal coach, feeling the pressure to be seen as not merely proficient in my performance but exemplary, and feeling the need to receive affirmation from my peers. As I took the stage for my first number and as the applause was dying down, I gazed rapidly around the room to see if Jim was there. And my eyes froze on Melinda; she had come to support me! This left me feeling both shame for how often I had let her down and, at the same time, overjoyed that she cared enough to show her support for my efforts.

It was not until after the recital had ended that I realized why Melinda had come, and I can't blame her; I deserved it. During the reception following my recital, people lined up to greet me as they were ushered into the parlor where cake and punch were being served. And then Melinda stepped into my peripheral line of sight, and I actually was glad to see her—just to know she was all right. Wondering how to greet her, what to say to someone I'd wounded so much, caused me to become quite nervous. With just enough anticipation and adrenaline to get me through the awkwardness of the moment, I simply said, "Thanks for coming."

And then she introduced me to her date.

She had brought a date to my senior recital! What I probably should've felt was anger or hurt, but what I felt was *thank you*. I felt grateful that she had given me what I knew I deserved. I felt thankful that somehow in that moment, I'd been repaid for my cruelty, and now we were somehow even. What I didn't find out until later was that Melinda had brought a date just to make me jealous. What it did for me, as weird as it sounds, was give me permission to lighten up on myself concerning my past with Melinda.

For the rest of that semester, I continued to find some solace in my emotional dependency on Jim and decided, stupidly so, to try just *one more time* with Melinda. Dating for the last few weeks of school, we had brief moments where we seemed to click—at least as friends. As graduation drew ever closer, the all-too-familiar pressure of such a momentous event began to weigh on me. With the real world quickly approaching came the real-world reality that the next step in my and Melinda's relationship was to decide whether or not to commit to each other for something more. I couldn't believe I was actually contemplating marriage, but I was. And that realization led me to one of the worst moments of my life.

The day before Melinda was to go home to Dallas for the summer and then on to graduate school, I told her I needed to speak with her about something important. With much anticipation, she met me, and we began to talk. As apparent as her excitement was over what she anticipated I would be speaking with her about, so too was the deep wounding that flooded her face as I took the conversation to that place we had been far too many times before.

"Melinda, I know you think I must be nuts for the way I've treated you in the past, but there's a reason for my behavior. There are things about me I can never tell you. Just trust me. You'll be better off without me. I want you to know I care deeply enough for you to say this to you."

Already beginning to sob, she literally fell apart, wailing in despair as I said, "I never want to see you again. You'll be better off without me."

I watched her as she walked away in despair. I ached with anguish over what I'd just done, but I'd honestly convinced myself that this was truly the best thing for both of us. And, as had been in all the downward spirals I'd already experienced in life, the emotional trauma I'd just created sent me once again longing for love in ways that were never intended to meet that longing.

I had to find Jim.

THE SUMMER OF LOVE?

It is with great difficulty that I even write this chapter. I find myself in the strange position of needing to tell my story yet needing to protect those I was involved with. What follows has been altered—both names and specifics of encounters—in order to convey my feelings and at the time preserve the dignity of others.

After Melinda and I broke up, Jim became the focus of my life. Our relationship was not sexual at all for many months. My regard for this man was built on the respect I saw others give to him based on his immense talent. He was an absolutely superb songwriter, destined for a big and bright future. Me, feeling utterly inadequate to write a song due to the discouragement I'd received my freshman year, held Jim and his gift in highest regard.

Upon graduation, I'd been in a quandary as to what I would do, but that question was answered when I was asked to be on a promotional team for the university. We were actually a musical quartet–two men and two women—that traveled the nation giving concerts and creating awareness of the university in the process. We were accompanied by a husband-and-wife team who handled all the driving and logistics. Since the team was based in Oklahoma and Jim was from Oklahoma, I knew I'd be able to spend time with him during the summer. I would have access to my friend *and* get to travel all over the country! It was a grand time in my life . . . at first.

Having not been out of Oklahoma but a handful of times during my college career, I couldn't wait for the van to be loaded and to hit the road. It was on our first trip that I discovered the vast expanse of the US in ways I'd only imagined before. What a joy and what a refreshing thing it was the day we set out for the Great Plains, from Oklahoma northward, all the way to North Dakota. While others saw only boring flatland, I saw grandeur and wondered what it must've taken to survive in such a harsh environment in olden days. Though at times the landscape did appear very flat and the drive grew monotonous at times, I began to see beyond the surface in ways that would keep my mind encouraged through some very quickly approaching dark times.

Passing through Kansas, I saw abandoned farmhouses next to once-grand barns, now falling into disrepair and dilapidation. With each farmhouse, I imagined who might've lived there in days gone by, wondered what their lives might've been like, and queried myself as to who might be buried beneath the tombstones nearby. At times I imagined children running in the fields, little girls in their spin-around dresses and little boys with pretend guns chasing one another through the waves of wheat. With each well, I conjured up images of hard-working women slogging water from the well into the house just to sustain their precious families; and with each crumbling silo, I imagined men who worked their fingers to the bone just to put away enough harvest to keep their families and livestock alive for one more winter. For once I was not focused on my performance and was learning to enjoy life.

Of course, those moments of daydreaming were brought to an end with each place we stopped to perform. Though we were doing religious music, I felt like such a hypocrite—singing words that were meant to encourage others while they condemned me! In other words, I was singing one thing but living another. Once again, performance ruled the day in my mind, which made me long for companionship, for someone just to talk to who might understand. This, in turn, caused me to think about Jim. Would I be able to spend time with him when I was home? Would he still feel the same way about me? Would he be there for me? Was he thinking about me?

As soon as I got back into town from that first trip, I went to see him. He seemed genuinely excited to see me. He welcomed me to spend the night with him, which made my heart leap! That meant he *wanted* to be with me! That meant he *enjoyed* being with me! That meant I was *worth* something to him. I felt valued for just being *me*. As we talked into the night, our conversation grew deep and covered a variety of subjects. Like two explorers just setting out to discover what the meaning of life truly was, we embarked on a deeply spiritual and philosophical journey of self-discovery. That first night I slept with a peace and confidence I'd not felt in quite some time, if ever.

During the day I'd practice with the other team members. It was exhilarating to be part of a team sanctioned by the university and to be regarded as special enough to represent the institution to others. Preparation was rigorous at times since we all wanted to perform with excellence, but I thoroughly enjoyed these practice times. What got me through the long days of rehearsal was the joy in knowing I'd get to spend time with Jim at night.

The next night began the same as the one before. As usual, the reality that in the morning I'd be embarking on another trip made me anxious to have a good night with my friend. I at once was both encouraged yet discouraged—encouraged that we'd be able to talk again, yet discouraged that we'd have to be separated again. I had become so dependent on Jim that he could've asked me to do anything, and I'd have done it to prove my love and loyalty to him.

What I didn't recognize was that Jim was also becoming dependent on me.   While I needed him to fill the voids in my life, he needed me to fill the voids in his. And while that sounds good in theory, those voids were never intended to be filled in the ways we were trying to fill them. I was in fact trying to fill the emptiness of my life and brokenness that only God could truly ever satisfy. Trying to meet one's needs in ways they were never meant to be met is like trying to put out a fire with gasoline. It *looks* like water, but it explodes with disastrous results. And my life was about to become a raging inferno!

As we talked into the night, our conversation once again went into deep places. Our honest desire was to discover who we truly were. I think this is quite common among college graduates or anyone facing a crossroads in life—to know who we truly are and why we even exist. Knowing I had to leave early the next morning, I shared my heart deeply and freely, still not confident enough to reveal the same-sex attraction I was trying to suppress although I certainly skirted the edges of that abyss that night.

Talking well into the wee hours of the morning, I finally expressed my need for sleep—that I had to get up early and that my body ached from the long hours of rehearsal and being squeezed into a van. Innocently, Jim offered to rub my back, and that sounded great to me. Believe it or not, I still wasn't thinking in sexual terms when he made the offer. The sexuality of the moment didn't strike me until he asked me if I'd be comfortable with him rubbing my butt. It was in that moment that everything changed in our relationship.

I'd never imagined being in a relationship with another man. Growing from an innocent flame of friendship into a raging fire of sexual experimentation, our relationship became all-consuming in my heart that night. It's one thing to have an emotional dependency on another man; it's quite another to have the added connection of sexual intimacy to cement the bond. Without knowing it, we'd crossed into a realm that is one of the most difficult to break: two men, bound by emotions, by sexual depravity and perversion, by the feeding of lust in a manner never intended. We'd bought into the lie that says "man is the utmost" and "whatever feels good, do it, as long as it hurts no one else." We were, in actuality, making each other an idol!

These encounters continued all summer. As soon as I got into town, I headed for him. Plunging headlong into deep and passionate talks about who we truly were and why we were here helped to ease the conflict I felt in my mind. As silly as it may sound, I was at once sexually fulfilled yet equally appalled at the perversion we were indulging in. My definition of perversion now is this: using something God intended for a holy purpose in a manner it was never intended. As much as I enjoyed the sexual act, I was consumed with the reality that no matter how I looked at our bodies, common sense—logic—told me that the two were never intended to be together in the manner we were indulging ourselves in.

Jim could sense my utter shame after each session and finally confronted me with it one night. "Why don't you just say it?" he asked.

"Say what?" I countered.

"You're a homosexual. You're *gay*."

The statement stunned me. Literally silenced me in every way. Like suddenly finding oneself standing utterly alone in a barren land with no end in sight. I felt completely hopeless to ever change. And that night, for the first time, I confessed to another person, "I am a homosexual. I am gay."

Odd as it sounds, I found peace in that moment. Simply affirming who I thought I was seemed to take so much pressure off my mind. This opened the door to much more than I'd bargained for. Soon I was thinking things that had never before crossed my mind.

It feels liberating to finally know who I am.

This is why I've never had peace before. I've been fighting against something I should've been embracing all along.

No one can fulfill a man better than another man. We know one another's bodies so well because they're the same as ours.

Thoughts about changing had been replaced with thoughts such as *Why would anyone want me to change who I was born to be? How can someone who's never experienced sex with someone of the same gender even know what they're talking about?* The enemy had effectively cut me off from hope, and I'd fallen headlong into the trap.

But there was a problem. The peace I felt in those first few days began to fade as the summer wore on. Jim and I verbally expressed our love for each other, but the more we indulged each other physically and emotionally, the more used I began to feel. And the more used I began to feel, the more bitterness I began to feel toward the one I was supposed to love. And the morbid reality that hit me squarely in the face was this: I'm using Jim just as much as he's using me. This realization led me to question everything I thought I'd finally come to terms with.

Is this all there is?

What is real love?

Feeling so deeply entrenched in this life now, I saw no way out. Assuming God had given up on me, I began to sink once again into a deep depression. This was truly one of the darkest episodes of my life. Gay, but not wanting to be. With someone, but feeling utterly alone. Emotionally dependent on another. Feeling used. Being the user. Like a boulder being shaken loose from the surrounding earth and tumbling helplessly into oblivion is how I felt. In my heart of hearts, I knew I needed to break things off with Jim, but in my heart of hearts, I didn't see how I could live without him. Not knowing what else to do, I simply fell apart and cried out in a shameful whimper of a whisper into what I assumed was thin air, "God, help me."

And then the phone rang.

THE RIDE BEGINS

As I had done so many times in the past, I cried out to God, hoping I could perform my way back into His good graces. In desperation, I cut off my relationship with Jim and decided to give God another chance. Pretty big of me, right? Although God had not intervened in my life while at OBU (at least from my point of view), I got the bright idea that maybe, just maybe, He would meet me and fix me if I went to seminary. At this stage of the game, I didn't see how it could hurt. After all, I'd already tried suicide—might as well try seminary. I enrolled and was going to be rooming with Reggie, a non-gay buddy of mine from my OBU days and a dear friend to this day. I had determined my future; things were going to be good.

That's when the phone rang.

On the other end of the line was a friend I'd known while at OBU. Chuck had graduated a year before me. Talented beyond measure, he was someone I respected greatly. It was exciting to hear from him. Assuming he was calling to catch up, I was somewhat taken aback when the conversation went far beyond surface pleasantries and plunged right into the deep end of spirituality.

"Dennis, the reason I'm calling you is this. The Lord's been speaking to me about you."

Although Chuck couldn't tell, his statement sent fear into my mind. Had he discerned my struggle? Was he about to confront me?

To this point in my life, God had not spoken to ME about me, so what was he saying to this guy?!

"Actually, the Lord came to me in a dream," he said.

A dream? Really? Had my friend lost his mind? God doesn't speak to people anymore—if He ever did. Why would He speak to someone else about me? But He had my attention.

"The Lord came to me in a dream and showed me that He would give you many, many songs. He showed me that people all over the world would be singing your songs one day."

I was speechless. Like a flood rushing into my mind were the words I'd heard uttered to me my freshman year in college when I went to the head of the Theory and Composition Department at OBU and had been told, "We have only a few positions in this department; we reserve them for people we see potential in, and we simply do not see any such potential in you. Based on your auditions and abilities demonstrated thus far, I must say no."

Chuck went on. "I know this is difficult to believe, but my mother, Beverly, had the same dream this week about you, and we don't believe it to be mere coincidence. We believe the Holy Spirit has spoken this to us, and we've been talking about what to do with what we've dreamed."

I was stunned with the weirdness I felt about people who claimed to hear God speak, yet sat on the edge of my proverbial seat with anticipation at where Chuck was going with all this "crazy talk."

"Dennis, we'd like to invite you to move in with us and give God a chance to work this in your life. In fact, I have a vision for creating a trio with you and Johnnie Ann. We could sing your music together. My mom is willing to put up the money to purchase a keyboard and a sound system. What do you think?"

I asked him to give me some time to think and pray about what he was asking me to do. Should I forego seminary and risk finding my freedom, or could I find freedom by moving to Oklahoma City with my friend and his mom? After saying goodbye to Chuck, I called my mom and told her about the opportunity to move into a place rent-free and work toward a career in music. Her response came quicker than I had anticipated. "I think you should take time to pursue your dream. You can always go back to seminary. I think time off from school would be a good thing for you. You've got your college degree; you'll find a job quickly."

Three days before I was to enter seminary, I called Chuck and told him I'd take him up on his offer. That same day, I had to call my friend, Reggie, and tell him that I wouldn't be attending seminary after all. After settling in, the job search was on. I applied at music stores. I applied at grocery stores. I applied for any job I could find. After a couple of weeks of fruitless job searching, I received a call from another friend I had known while at OBU. He told me of a job opening at a new hotel in downtown Oklahoma City where I could make a ton of money as a bellman, especially if I would work on weekends and be willing to go to the rooms of certain men and do whatever they needed. He told me I could make up to five hundred dollars a night or more.

Whatever they needed? The implication sank in. Having to pay back my school loans was already weighing heavily on my mind, so much so that the pressure to attain money overrode the pressure to remain pure. As I got into my car and headed for my interview downtown, I consciously shut out the convicting thoughts that had begun to hound me since consenting to do the interview. *Is this truly best for you? Is this truly pleasing to the Lord? What will you say if anyone asks you what you do? How will you explain away your sin?*

Just as loudly were the thoughts from the other direction. *Who's going to find out? How can you turn down an offer where you can make up to five hundred dollars or more a night? How can you disregard such a great opportunity? Are you a fool?*

Once again, I was hearing voices in my head, and once again, I refused to acknowledge that the war being waged for my mind might just be as simple as good versus evil—as simple as God versus Satan. I discounted the possibility that it might be God trying to get my attention. To shut out my thoughts, I quickly turned on the radio, which had been tuned to a popular Christian radio station. As the music began, the voice I heard was very familiar. While the voice of Keith Green was both soothing and convicting, a shudder went down my spine with the words I heard pouring out of those tiny car speakers. Like a knife piercing the hardness of my heart and mind, Keith sang, "Unless the Lord builds the house, they labor in vain to try at all building anything not according to His call. Unless the Lord wants it done, you'd better not work another day building anything that'll stand in His way."

As the words were etched into my mind, I began to shake and my body went cold. I immediately turned the car around and didn't go to the interview. It was in that moment that I knew God was real and that He was trying to get my attention. I knew that there must be hope for me for such a big and distant God to suddenly intervene in my life in such a profound way. Broken and humbled, I walked back into the house and decided I would look for a job elsewhere—that God must have something for me to have taken such drastic steps to stop me in my tracks as He had just done.

My thoughts went back to something my mom had told me a few weeks earlier when I'd asked her if I should go to seminary. She had said that I'd find a job quickly. After the job interview incident, I decided I couldn't be picky or pretentious about finding a job, so I broadened my search and found that my mom had been right. I did find a job quickly—driving a school bus for the local school district. (A bachelor's degree in church music doesn't open one's job selection to a very wide field.) Although the job seemed somehow "beneath" me (there's that pride again), God was about to take me on the most incredible journey of my life. And I was in no way prepared for the whirlwind of a roller coaster ride it was about to become.

SINGING MY WAY TO SANITY

I'm convinced that God has a wonderful sense of humor because I can look back on my life now and see His hand and laugh about all He brought me through. He took an arrogant, haughty-minded musician and put him smack-dab on a school bus with screaming kids. Now *that's* funny! I wish I'd had eyes to see His hand at work and ears to hear the direction of His voice. At best, I was like a lamb being led to slaughter by the enemy, yet a little lost lamb being pursued by a very jealous and vigilant Shepherd.

Humiliation was a feeling I'd grown quite accustomed to, yet I still winced whenever someone would ask me what I did for a living. Oh, how much I wanted to say I was a big wig musician at some hoity-toity church—but no, I was relegated to apologizing for being a lowly bus driver for a bunch of kids who couldn't care less that I even existed. Pride comes before a fall, but falling isn't bad if you fall in the right place. And without knowing it, I was about to fall all right.

I had hours to kill between my morning and afternoon bus routes, and time on one's hands can be a breeding ground for insane thoughts. Like being caught in some vicious and cosmic holy war for my mind, the thoughts of same-sex attraction were my constant companion, tugging at my mind, reminding me of the words I'd spoken to myself not so long ago: *You were born this way. Stop fighting, and just be who you were meant to be.*

The other party involved in the battle for my thoughts came through the many encouraging words spoken to me almost daily by my friend, Chuck. He would often tell me things God was speaking to him about me. Chuck's words were life to me whenever he was around, but those hours between bus routes were an entirely different story. All I could hear were the words of allure calling me back to finding peace and solace in the arms of another man. It was almost too much for my mind to bear. I honestly thought I was losing my mind, so fierce was the battle.

I don't recall what triggered it, but in the midst of my daily turmoil—whether to pursue homosexuality or to pursue God—I suddenly recalled a story I'd heard from my childhood that brought a tinge of sanity to my mind. Though I didn't understand why, I recalled how God had allowed an evil spirit to torment Saul, the King of Israel. And I remembered how King Saul had sent for the shepherd boy, David, to help drive away the evil spirit.

> So it came about whenever the evil spirit from God came to Saul, David would take the harp and play it with his hand; and Saul would be refreshed and be well, and the evil spirit would depart from him (1 Samuel 16:23 NASB).

In that moment, a sane thought went through my mind. *If God did that for King Saul, then I would do that for myself!* My reasoning? David was known for being a writer of many of the Psalms found in the Bible. David would simply worship God, and the enemy would flee! I imagined that when David was a small boy tending his father's sheep, there were good reasons why he had developed a heart and an attitude of worship. A constant threat to those defenseless sheep were the wild bears and lions that roamed about in those days. David must've grown to trust God to such a degree that his fear was overcome by God's love. And taking it a step further, I reasoned that perhaps God could find a place for me in His heart since He had done so for David—the same David who had committed adultery; the same David who had his own friend, Uriah, murdered to cover up the affair; and yet the same David who is exalted in Scripture as being "a man after God's own heart." According to Acts 22:13, the Lord said, "I HAVE FOUND DAVID, the son of Jesse, A MAN AFTER MY HEART, who will do all My will." It was with that realization that I began to believe that if God could do that for David, He could do it for me.

My routine from that point on was to finish my route as quickly as I could in the morning so I could get to Chuck's piano! Once there, I would simply open up my Bible to Psalm 1 and begin singing. Making up my own melodies, I would sing and sing and sing until it was time for my afternoon bus route to begin. And just as God had done for King Saul, He used the words of the psalmists to keep the lies of the enemy at bay in my mind. It was during those long sessions of worship that I began to discover some things about the Word of God that I'd somehow missed as a child. The psalmists wrote some pretty horrendous things about how they felt—things that were quite contrary to the nature and goodness of God. Things like . . .

> O daughter of Babylon, you devastated one,
> How blessed will be the one who repays you
> With the recompense with which you have repaid us.
> How blessed will be the one who seizes and dashes
>   your little ones
> Against the rock (Psalm 137:8-9 NASB).

How blessed will be the one who seizes and dashes their little ones against the rocks? How had I never seen that before? How could a holy man of God utter such hateful words about the children of another—whether the children of his enemy or not?! And then it dawned on me as I would again sing through the Psalms as a part of my daily routine—those words were simply an expression of how the writer felt, not necessarily how he was supposed to respond! In other words, God could handle my feelings if I would simply be honest enough to confess them to Him. Just look at the words of the great King David expressing his own feelings, and you'll see how I began to identify with him on such a deeply profound level.

> But I am a worm and not a man,
> A reproach of men and despised by the people.
> All who see me sneer at me;
> They separate with the lip, they wag the head (Psalm
>   22:5-6 NASB).

It didn't take long for me to decide that if David could be so bluntly honest with God, then so could I! After singing through the Psalms, it began to dawn on me as well that maybe, in spite of the discouragement I'd faced concerning writing songs while in college, I could actually write my own songs to God. In fact, as hard as I tried, I couldn't think of one song that dealt with homosexuality, so I began to write my own. Day after day, I'd sing through the Psalms then take time to write down my own heart's cry to God as deeply and emotionally and rawly as I'd perceived David and the other psalmists had done.

After many weeks of this routine, I got up the nerve to show Chuck one of the songs I'd written.

> A hungry thirsting stranger cries
> An empty burdened soul
> A hurt so deep it never heals
> The hurting sometimes shows
> Locked inside a puzzled mind
> Naked to his thoughts
> Too hurt to feel the sickness

Like stones among the rocks
(from the Dennis Jernigan song, FOR THE LEAST
   OF ME)

Soon, as in Chuck's initial dream, he, Johnnie, and I were singing the simple songs I was writing. We would gather each Tuesday evening for worship around the piano. We called these gatherings our campfire meetings because we stood around the piano and simply sang as if we were around a campfire. Though we didn't necessarily realize it at the time, we were all so very hungry for more of God—more of something than what life had brought to each of us—that we began to feel measures of healing and freedom seep into our broken lives.

As my friends began to encourage my songwriting, it was as if some great beast had been released from somewhere deep inside my soul. I imagined myself being a co-writer with King David and the other psalmists. I wrote with the mighty writers of church history. Asaph. The sons of Korah. Moses. Solomon. Ethan the Ezrahite. I could not wait to get to the piano each day and begin my routine. Soon the songs were pouring out of me at a level I could never have anticipated! I'm sure my friends were a bit overwhelmed at my newfound passion, but it felt liberating to release the things I'd been hiding. Even if I could never bring myself to share the true root of the hurts, at least I was acknowledging the hurt. My hope and assumption were that my friends were simply interpreting my emotional outpourings in song as an honest expression of the angst of a young soul in search of meaning . . . just as they were!

For the first time in a long time, I was feeling a bit victorious over same-sex thoughts and feelings. Some would say I was simply suppressing my thoughts. I've since come to understand that what I was doing was actually learning to exchange one set of thoughts— one way of thinking—for another. This process was put on the fast track with one simple statement by my friend, Chuck. Who would've thought all that I'd attained in a few short weeks would come crashing down with one innocent and grace-filled expression of love?

WHEN GOD SPOKE

"I need to talk with you," was all he said. I'd not expected to hear such gravity in his tone. Chuck's statement caught me so by surprise that I had no other option but to run. That night I could tell he had something on his mind just by the way he was extra-kind to me, extra-attentive to my feelings, extra-encouraging. After dinner, we settled in the living room and, as was typical for our evenings, we went to the piano to sing some of the songs I'd been writing. All was well in my mind. The music flowed easily. The atmosphere was peaceful and serene, like I didn't have a care in the world. And my friend was so gracious to me. Chuck was always kind in all his ways, but for some reason, he was extra-sensitive to my mood that night.

After singing a few songs, we began to talk. Talking with Chuck was always so freeing and refreshing, full of encouraging words as well as words of challenge. He was always challenging me to go deeper in the things of God, and he was very sensitive when it came to sharing things God had impressed upon his heart for me. I couldn't help but think of the dream that had set me on my current journey—the one that had sent me to live with him. So whenever Chuck said he felt God had something for him to share with me, I was all ears. And tonight was no different.

"I have something I need to share with you, Dennis," he began.

"Sure," I said. "Go ahead."

Hesitating for a few seconds, like a wise man does, weighing his thoughts with discernment as how best to express them, I could tell that whatever Chuck had to say to me was pressing down heavily upon his heart.

"I've heard some things about you."

I froze.

"What have you heard?" I asked.

I could now see anguish on Chuck's face but felt a deep compassion emanating from him as well. Looking me eye to eye, he said, "I know you're struggling with homosexuality."

In utter shock and disbelief that my secret had been spilled—and then filled with simultaneous rage and humiliation to know that my friend had heard the news from someone else—I burst from the room and out the front door, running as fast as I possibly could into the night. I ran and I ran and I ran, thinking all the while, *My life is over!* I ran in desperation. I ran on the adrenaline sent coursing through my body at the shame of being found out and confronted by one of my best friends. Crying and shaking and feeling completely humiliated, I continued to run for several minutes. And then I stopped.

As if a glass of cold, icy water had been suddenly thrown in my face, I was brought back to reality with this thought: *Where am I going? Where am I running to? What do I do now? I have no place left to turn.* My best friend, whose home and presence had been a refuge for me, was suddenly gone. Assuming that Chuck's reason for telling me he knew about my secret was because he would need me to leave his home, I decided to just not go back. But still the question—*Where do I go now?*—kept playing over and over in my mind.

Now sobbing uncontrollably, finding myself helpless and alone in the middle of a dark street in the middle of the night somehow seemed appropriate. Like the epitome of irony, the very thing I longed for, to be known completely, was the very thing that had now ushered me into what was the deepest abyss my soul had ever descended. I thought I'd felt hopeless before, but NOW I knew

I'd reached the end of the road. Alone. Abandoned. Helpless. Without hope. And I stood there frozen at the edge of a cliff.

I didn't know I could cry so deeply. I didn't know I could still feel so deeply. I had not expected this tonight; the night had been going so well. Why did it have to end this way? Wailing now, I began to cry out, "Why, Lord? Why?" and then the moaning grew deeper as the cry changed to, "Father, if you are real, if You are even there, I need You to speak to me! If ever I've needed you, it's now! Please speak to me!"

Somehow, simply uttering those words calmed my soul. Somehow, admitting I was helpless brought me to the place of complete brokenness and humility. Somehow, I knew I had no other hope if He didn't speak. And it didn't take long.

The night was dark, yet the sky was bright, illuminated by a full moon. I hadn't noticed the moon until that moment, so consumed with my pain had I been. So self-focused that I hadn't noticed the two clouds in the sky that now drew my attention. Without realizing what I was doing, I began thinking about my days as a child out on the farm when I would just lie down in the grass and watch the clouds go by. Many hours had been been spent looking to the clouds for images and shapes of creatures and people. I recalled dinosaurs and horses, sailing ships and serpents. For a few brief seconds, I was somehow taken back to those days. To feel the innocence and wonder of a child was soothing to my grieving soul. And then I was shaken back to the present reality—to the two clouds, their shapes very evident in the moonlit sky.

At first I couldn't believe what I was seeing. Didn't want to put my hope in something not real. But the clouds WERE real and had very definite shapes. Recognizable shapes. Life-shaking shapes. And as if taken by unseen hands, my face was directed to look fully at what was transpiring in the heavens above me.

I was first drawn to the larger of the two clouds. There was no mistaking the image of an old man with a beard. With definition of features, the face was loving and welcoming and inviting.

I couldn't release my gaze on the figure; it was so full of love and acceptance. And then my face was directed to the smaller cloud. Amazed at what I was seeing, this cloud looked like a small lamb. A sheep. A wounded sheep in need of love and care. And as if on some cosmic cue, the old man cloud began to catch up to the little lamb cloud as if it were pursuing the broken little sheep. And then the old man cloud began to consume the little lamb cloud within itself! They became ONE! I couldn't believe what I was seeing. But hadn't I just asked the Lord to speak to me? And now this?!

Overwhelmed by all manner of GOOD thoughts, I started to calm down, and peace began to flood my mind. Suddenly I knew what my Father was saying: "This is what I want to do with and for you, son. I want to consume you. Consume your brokenness. Love you. Bind up your wounds. Heal your broken heart."

It was in that moment that I heard, not in an audible voice but rather in an impression on my mind, "Go back and face your friend. He's waiting for you. You can trust Me." So I went back home. It was a long walk, not because of the distance but because I was so afraid of what my friend might say and do. Even though I felt I'd just heard the Lord speak to me, I was still so full of fear, I could hardly function. All I know is that somehow the Lord gave me the strength to head home.

Approaching the door, I thought I'd be able to sneak in without Chuck noticing, but he hadn't moved from where I'd last seen him. He'd been waiting all that time. Just that realization—that he had waited—sent waves of peace through my veins. It's one thing for someone to tell you he loves you; quite another for the person to prove his love. In that moment, I gained a deeper understanding of what real love was supposed to look like. Real loves requires the laying down of life. Sacrifice. And Chuck was about to lay down his life for me in a deeply profound way.

Slinking into the room, head bowed dejectedly, I could not bring myself to even look at him, so wracked with shame was I. In his wisdom, my friend did not try to get me to look him right in the eye, but wisely waited to allow the honesty of the moment and the depth of his love and commitment restore me to a feeling of pure acceptance, void of shame.

He simply asked me to sit down because he had something he wanted to share with me. Expecting complete rejection, I girded myself for the worst. But with the very tone of his voice and the compassion with which he spoke, I was set immediately at ease as I took my seat near him.

"Dennis," he began. "I'll be honest with you. I don't know how to help you. All I know is I know the answer."

At once I was flooded with feelings of hope, and I began to let my guard down. "You know the answer? What's the answer?"

His reply was short and to the point: "Jesus is the Answer."

As I sat there stunned and actually a bit incredulous in attitude, I repeated, "Jesus is the Answer?! I've heard that my whole life! I've asked Him to change me time and time again, and nothing's ever happened! How is Jesus the Answer? I've heard it all before."

"Not like this, you haven't," he declared confidently.

"What do you mean?" I asked.

What he said next took my breath away, and still does to this day whenever I remember that moment. "Though I don't know any magic formula or know what steps might be required for your freedom from this, I do believe Jesus is the Answer. And here's what I mean by that. I believe so much that He's what you need to be free that I'm willing to walk toward Jesus with you for as long as it takes, whatever it takes. When you fall down, I'll not kick you. I'll not say I told you so. You know what I'll do? I'll help you up every time."

By now, my tears had again begun to flow. As if being bathed in pure love and acceptance, though I did not know it at the time, I was having a real-life, personal demonstration of the act of love, the laying down of life. But he wasn't quite through.

"Dennis, not only will I walk with you as long as it takes. If you need a shoulder to cry on, use mine. If you need someone to yell at when the frustration grows too burdensome, yell at me; I can handle it. Let's just walk toward Jesus together."

It was in that moment that God restored hope in my soul, and it began to burn like a fire within me. As never before, I began to seek Jesus, but not yet understanding that God's love for me was in no way connected to my performance. At least now I didn't feel so alone. Finally, I had someone who, though they might not have gone through exactly what I'd gone through in my life, was sensitive enough to walk through the recovery of a broken heart with me.

Little did I know it, but that encounter with my friend was the setup for a bombshell about to explode in my life—an explosion of love like I'd never imagined even possible for someone like me.

P.S. By the way, Chuck kept his word. He has walked toward Jesus with me for the past thirty-two years. Love looks like my friend, Chuck.

WHEN I CAME OUT

After the encounter with Chuck—after having the love of Christ demonstrated to me in such a tangible way—I was once again hopeful that change was possible. Still, my belief that people regarded homosexuality as the worst of the worst when it came to categorizing sin clouded everything, especially how I viewed myself and how I perceived everyone would think of me should they discover my secret. At least Chuck's response had given me a glimmer of hope, something to hang on to.

During the fall of 1981, I was well into my daily routine: get up; drive my morning bus route; sing through a series of Psalms; write my own psalms to God; do my afternoon bus route; eat dinner with Chuck and his mom; show Chuck any new songs I'd received that day; go to bed thinking about how and when freedom might come to me; dream of adventure, capture, and liberation; wake feeling rescued; repeat. It was during this period of my life when I began to practice the discipline of worship and communion with God, even though I didn't yet really know what that meant. Had no clue as to exactly how intimately and how deeply God could possibly love me. In a sense, I was still performing for God's approval. Little did I know that the performance was about to come to an end. Soon I would be seeking intimacy with God out of sheer love rather than for what I could gain from Him.

In November of that year, I heard that my favorite band, 2nd Chapter of Acts, was going to be in concert later in the month. Of course, I was going to be there if at all possible! I'd just bought their new album *Rejoice!* and had already memorized most of the songs. As the day approached, my heart began to fill with joy and gratitude that the band God had used to get me through college was now going to be in my neck of the woods. Because I knew they'd not only be doing songs from the new recording but would also be doing music from their earlier days, I got the bright idea to record the evening's events myself.

I knew in my heart that to record a concert was illegal, but I justified my actions by telling myself no one would care, no one would even notice, that it wouldn't affect their sales. The truth is, it was stealing, and stealing is sin. But God used even my sin to bring healing to my life. He had mercy on me even when I willfully robbed from this band in that, though I didn't know it at the time, He was going to allow me to record my own deliverance, that very moment when healing began to flood my heart and mind, the very instant when new life was birthed in my innermost being.

On November 7, 1981, I arrived at Lloyd Noble Center, the basketball arena on the campus of the University of Oklahoma in Norman, Oklahoma. I made my way into the arena, successfully hiding the three blank cassette tapes and a small cassette tape recorder. My plan? To get a three-album set that night! Little did I know of all that was about to transpire. All I knew was that something about the honesty of this music was able to penetrate my soul like no other. Something about the passion of these three singers was able to make me feel wanted and special and needed, not alone. Something about the way they spoke between songs took the concert out of the realm of performance and set the most deeply satisfying atmosphere of worship, of God-awareness, I had ever known!

And the concert began. Almost forgetting to reach beneath my seat to press the record and play buttons, I was immediately ushered into another place in my heart and mind. Singing songs from the new album, the band went flawlessly from song to song. I was awed at Matthew's vocal range and clarity. I was mesmerized as I hung on every word I knew Annie had written. As then-pregnant Nellie sang *Mountain Tops,* I could see and feel everything she was so beautifully trying to convey. It was as if she was singing my heart.

> The mountain tops are not as tall
> The valleys seem to be getting small
> Still the river rolls deep inside me
> Take the dreams that didn't grow
> And visions that melted in the snow
> Take away my laugh
> Still I'll climb the pathway home
>
> With my hand in your hand
> My life in your life
> My spirit will rise
> Until I see the rainbow
> *Words & Music: Annie Herring*
> *Used by Permission*

With each song, I was being ushered into an awareness I still could not quite get myself to believe—that maybe God DID have a plan for me; maybe He COULD make a way out of this vast mountainous wilderness, my homosexuality. Still unaware that God was indeed at work engineering a once-in-a-lifetime event just for me, I sang along with every word, making their prayers my prayers, making their declarations my declarations. It didn't dawn on me until later that during such moments of intense revelry I WAS free. My entire being—thoughts, attitudes, emotions, and body—were transported momentarily to a place where homosexuality *had* no place. It gives me chills to think about all that entails for me now as it relates to where I am in the here and now.

And then, Annie began the introduction to one of my favorite 2nd Chapter songs of all time. Written in my favorite key of all time, D-flat, the very familiar strains of the song began, and my heart began to melt into ecstasy of God's hope as the lush three-part harmonies of the siblings kicked into gear on the chorus.

So why should I worry?
Why should I fret?
'Cause I've got a Mansion Builder
Who ain't through with me yet
Words & Music: Annie Herring
Used with Permission.

As the song came to a close, I couldn't help but relish the feelings of hope and peace that flooded my soul. And, dare I say, feelings of being *loved?* With 4,500 people in the audience that night, imagine my surprise when Annie began to speak to ME! At least that's what it felt like. Like someone opening my most intimate mail and reading it aloud to the entire world was how the things she began to speak felt to me. And since I have the recording to refer to, I will let you in on what the power of Holy Spirit-inspired words did for my entire being that night.

I know that tonight that there are many of you here who have gone through things that have hurt you deeply. And it's not like you're not willing to give those things to Jesus; it's just that you've never had the opportunity to. Well, tonight we're going to get rid of all of our hurts. Tonight we're going to allow Him to take up residence in areas where we have kept Him out because we weren't aware of the fact that we were closing Him out. But I believe the Holy Spirit has done a work in your heart tonight to open up areas where His light hasn't shined for a long time . . . or never has shined. We are very complex people. But we need to choose to let His light shine in all those rooms in our heart. And I know that the Lord is showing me that there are many of you tonight that are broken-hearted. And many of you have gone through—well, things that you never thought you'd have to go through. And you need to be set free tonight. The Lord wants to heal your mind and your heart.

The way that we're going to get rid of all the things inside of us—and we ALL have something to get rid of because we are all being built. We are in the same body. The way we're going to get rid of those things tonight is we're going to put our hands up before us like this (she then extends her hands out in front of her, palms up, like receiving a gift from someone else), and we're going to place those things right there, and we're going to GIVE them to the Lord while we sing this song. We're going to lift those things to the Lord and give them away. And then while our hands are up and empty—lifting our hands is a sign of surrender—we're surrendering those things to the Lord. And after we give them to Him and our hands are empty, we're going to receive from Him whatever gift it is that He wants to give us tonight. And I guarantee you, it's a good gift. You have nothing to be afraid of. He   only wants what's best for you.

So, it's sort of like Christmas. We're going to give away something, and we're going to receive from Him a gift. And there's a gift for each one of us with our name on it. So, let's prepare ourselves, and let's let Him have our hearts. You ready to sing?

Some of you aren't ready. You're still like this (arms folded). It doesn't work. You choose. We are people of choice, and you choose to get rid of these things. Receive from Him tonight. You ready? Yeah. Okay. Here we go. Everybody sing.

Stunning. She had spoken directly to me. How had she known of the depth of my hurt, or that I'd never had the opportunity to give the hurts away? That I didn't even know HOW to give them away? Until that moment I thought my sin, homosexuality, was my identity—that my sin was too vile for Jesus to take upon the cross! How had she known of the hidden rooms in my heart? How could she possibly have known that I'd gone through things in my life I never thought I would go through? How could anyone know of the broken heart I had carried for so long? And how dare she say it was simply a choice? I had not chosen the things that tempted me! I had not chosen to be victimized! I had not chosen to be betrayed!

"You choose. We are people of choice."

As the trio sang, those words began to haunt my mind, echoing over and over again, mixing with the precious words of the simple chorus, "Why should I worry? Why should I fret? I've got a Mansion Builder Who ain't through with me yet," leading me to the realization that I indeed DID have a choice in the matter. I could choose to believe that homosexuality was my destiny and identity, or I could choose to believe that God had something better for me— freedom from sin, victory over temptation, and a purpose and destiny apart from and soaring over homosexuality.

The song took all of thirty seconds to sing, but I lived a lifetime of redemption in those thirty seconds. Like giving away a gift on Christmas morning, I did the simplest thing I could think of; I simply gave homosexuality to Jesus. I had never done that before! Never crossed my mind that He would dare come near it. Yet somehow I knew now was the time to simply give it to Jesus.

Placing homosexuality on His shoulders, placing the powerlessness I felt toward that temptation on His shoulders, placing all the willfully sinful things I'd ever done on His shoulders, I saw myself crucified with Christ. I saw me dead and in the grave. I saw Jesus risen and standing at the opening of the tomb, simply extending a hand to me, saying, "Dennis Jernigan, come forth!"

As the song played and this vision unfolded before my eyes, I began to understand the gift God had for me in that moment. Unexpected feelings of being loved, of being lovable, began to flood my entire being. It was as if He was saying to me, "I love you right where you are, son! But I love you enough to not leave you there! Come with Me! I'll show you who I intended you to be all along."

With the song coming to a close, all I could do was sob. In fact, on the recording, all I heard from that point on was the sound of beautiful singing being interrupted by the cries of a heart being broken by the sheer weight of God's forgiving, redeeming, unconditional, unfathomable, yet completely accessible love! Tears of freedom! Tears of acceptance based solely on someone's expression of worth! Tears caused at the realization that Dennis Jernigan was worth Jesus' own life!

Stunning. Life-changing. Altered forever.

I walked out of homosexuality that night and into the most wonderful adventure of my life—the living out of the healing and redemption I'd just experienced. I'm sure you have many questions at this point, and I don't blame you. Was my healing instantaneous? Was my healing a process? Did the temptation go away immediately? Am I tempted anymore?

This is where the story gets REALLY good. This is how I came out.

THE MAGIC FORMULA
FOR FREEDOM AND
OTHER MYTHS

I realize this book has just taken a deep turn into the spiritual realm. I urge you to bear with me; there's a very good reason for doing this. I'd gotten myself into quite a mess of a life, but through faith in Jesus Christ, I was able to allow Him to begin unraveling that mess, a process which continues to this day. He unraveled not only my belief that I was homosexual but an entire existence, proving to me along the way that with Him, NOTHING is impossible.

There is no magic formula for freedom from same-sex attraction, but there is a way out; I know because I found it, or perhaps it found me. Due to all I'd gone through in my life from my earliest sexual encounters to that night in November 1981, and due to the feelings of utter hopelessness I'd discovered in homosexuality in general, I decided to wipe the slate clean, start over. I would no longer allow my past failures or sexual temptations to define me. I would no longer allow my gay friends or the gay community to define me. I even determined that Dennis Jernigan would not get to define himself. That reduced the defining factors in my life to their lowest common denominator: God. Only my Maker would define me.

Those determinations meant I had to strip away everything that had previously crowded my mind for attention. I had to come to a basic understanding of my faith. God is God; I am not. He is the Potter; I am the clay. He is the Shepherd; I am the sheep. He is the Father; I am the child. He is my Maker; I was designed by Him; therefore, it stood to reason in my mind that going to anything other than my Maker to find my destiny and purpose for existence was foolishness. I needed to go directly to the source. If I had a problem with my car, I would never take it to the grocery store to get repairs done; I would go to the manufacturer. I would never take my broken laptop to the local ice cream store for repairs; I would look at the manual. I would go to the manufacturer.

What happened to me on the night of November 7, 1981, was that I was born again. By placing my faith in Christ, I was given a brand new identity. The old Dennis was crucified with Christ by faith. The old me was buried with Him by faith. The new me was raised to a brand-new life in and with and through faith in Christ! Faith transcends how I feel at any given moment. Faith transcends what others think or don't think of me at any given moment. Faith transcends even my circumstances. I began to look at my life from a whole new point of view. In an instant, I was completely changed. But change is a process.

Being made brand-new didn't erase my past. Being born again didn't cause the temptations to cease. Being born again didn't relieve me of the circumstances of life. Being born again simply gave me a proper foundation and worldview from which to operate. Being born again gave me the proper perspective on temptation and how my Father can use it to bring even deeper freedom to my soul. Being born again gave me a proper perspective as to how to face the circumstances of life rather than be overcome and overwhelmed by them.

The process looks a lot like Lazarus, the friend of Jesus, who had been dead and in the grave for several days. When Jesus got to the tomb of his friend, he simply said, "Lazarus, come forth," and

Lazarus walked out of the grave! He was alive—fully alive, gratefully alive, joyously alive. Yet Lazarus was not FREE even though he was now alive. Jesus said to those gathered in amazement around the risen man, "Loose from him the grave clothes." What were the grave clothes? Strips of material, like a mummy's wrappings, meant to bind and cover the body. As Lazarus began to walk toward Jesus, people began helping him unravel the things that once defined him in death but now only served to bind him in life. I decided on November 7, 1981, that I would simply walk toward Jesus and trust Him and those He sent to help me unravel the mess of my past, a past I had formerly allowed to define me!

It suddenly became apparent to me that since childhood I had believed a vast number of lies about myself, lies planted in my mind concerning my sexual identity, my worth, my talents, my personality, my character, and everything about me, it seemed. I could no longer trust anyone from my past to help me because I reasoned they were in the same predicament as I was. In that moment, I decided I would go to the Word of God, the manual, and to Father God Himself in intimate prayer and worship—not to discover who I was but rather to discover who He was! It made sense to me that if by faith I was truly His son, then His spiritual DNA flowed through my veins. So in order to know who I was, I had to first find out Who He said HE was!

I discovered that He loved me right where I was, but that He loved me enough to not leave me there. I discovered that He takes more joy in MY presence than I could possibly take in His. I discovered that even when I was fully engaged in homosexual behavior, He thought I was worth dying for. I discovered that He could take even my failures, my wounds, and the things the Liar meant for evil and turn them around and use them for MY GOOD!

I began pouring my heart out to God in song and prayer. I began calling anything contrary to His Word a lie, and I promptly replaced it with the truth His Word revealed to me. Worship took on a whole new meaning for me. Worship was more than my singing into thin air to a being that may or may not be there. Worship became to me a practice of intimacy with God. In other words, I would run to Him and bare my heart to Him in honesty, saying, "Here is my heart, Father. Into me see." And in my faith I would hear Him say to me, "Son, here is My heart. Into Me see." He had exchanged my old life for His on the cross, and I had left that old guy in the grave. I walked out of that grave and smack-dab into the most liberating, fulfilling, and life-giving relationship I'd ever known. Up until this time in my life, I had viewed God as a cosmic policeman, watching me to see when I would mess up so He could swoop in and bop me on the head, but now I saw Him as the God Who so patiently waited for me, the God Who wanted me so much He gave everything He had and everything He was to make me His own. How could I NOT follow hard after that kind of love?!

When I discovered the battleground of my life was NOT my body but rather my mind, I began to take drastic steps to cleanse my mind, erasing every thought that came against the nature God had intended for me and replacing it with the truth according to HIS Word and HIS nature. Those steps will seem perhaps insane to you, but I knew I needed deep surgery and not just a simple bandage for the wounds of my life. The first thing I did was to burn every letter and picture and gift that had been given to me in the homosexual relationships I had been a part of. My reason? I had to cut all emotional ties that did not jibe with my relationship with God.

From 1981 until 1993, I cut out all music—Christian, secular, and otherwise—save for the music God was birthing in me. Cutting out TV and movies and any voice I deemed an obstacle between me and my God, I began to listen for what HE had to say to me through His Word; through other believers; and through His still, small voice. And like Lazarus, the old grave clothes—the things I used to think defined me—began to be ripped away.

When I was a child, I would throw the occasional tantrum. My mom would tell me, "That's just the Bristol in you." Meaning I was responding like my fiery, red-headed great-grandparents, the

Bristols. Meaning I could not help but be angry because that is "just the way I am." The Lord dealt with that one day when I lashed out in anger, and I heard His voice say in that moment of rage, "That's NOT who you are, son. Who told you you were an angry man? That anger is part of the old grave clothes that defined you as a dead man. Let's rip those away. See what's exposed now—that heart of peace I planted in you! Just *be* that, son."

After the night of November 7, 1981, my life became less about performing for acceptance and approval and more about learning to just *be*. The bouncing from one traumatic experience to the next was replaced by a constant flow of existence as I put into practice what Annie Herring had spoken that night—that we are people of choice. In other words, it dawned on me that, even if traumatic things DID happen to me, I still had a choice as to how I would respond to them. That was a game-changer for me!

Although it would take me seven more years to gain the confidence to share my story publicly, the seeds of healing, freedom, and restoration were planted in my heart and mind that night. People often ask me if my healing was instant or if it was a process. The answer is both. In an instant, I was completely and utterly changed from death to life, from old to new, from gay to straight, from darkness to light. But the process has been like Lazarus walking out of the tomb as I allowed the Father to loose from me the grave clothes that USED to define me, and I allowed myself to be defined by Him and Him alone.

Sounds too good to be true? Believe me, you can't make up a story like mine. I thought the events of November 7, 1981, were monumental—and they were—but what was about to come would rock my world and blow my mind even further than it had already been rocked and blown!

I'd given up on ever marrying or having a family, but God had other things in mind for me. He wanted me to be married . . . to a woman!

MARRIED ... TO A WOMAN!

As I was growing up, I often dreamed of marriage, but as time wore on and same-sex attraction took center stage in my mind, I had all but given up on ever being married to anyone, much less to a woman! But indeed, Father did have other plans for me. Content to be celibate—at least that's what I told myself—I always yearned for and believed that one day I would have a family; I just didn't see a way. For one thing, I didn't think a woman would want to have anything to do with someone who struggled with same-sex attraction. And for another, I didn't think my body would respond sexually to a woman since I'd not felt aroused by a female to this point.

After the night of the 2nd Chapter of Acts concert, my perception change about everything. My perception of God changed. My perception of others changed. My perception of myself changed. With each passing day of my new way of looking at life—that I should find my identity in Christ by walking intimately with Him— the lies I'd been believing began to be shattered by the truth of God's point of view. Suddenly having a foundation of truth from which to operate made dealing with temptation much easier. Knowing the things that tempted me had no power to define me gave me such power to continue the journey toward even more freedom.

So much healing was coming into my life that I was becoming more and more open to the reality that I COULD hear God speak to ME. It was during this period of my life when I began to trust Father with the most minute areas of my life. To get to know someone intimately, one must spend time with another in conversation, just asking simple questions. In the infancy of my faith, I would ask things like, "Lord, do you love me? Show me how much you love me." From there, I graduated to "Father, would you show me what to wear today? Would you guide me to specific passages of Your Word that deal with the issue of healing?" Asking such intimately mundane questions taught me how to listen for God's still, small voice. Once I began to feel confident with the little things, I graduated to the bigger matters of life, like marriage.

Many of my friends were getting engaged after college, so quite naturally, marriage was never far from my thoughts, especially as I recalled the dreams of my youth of one day having a wife and children. These thoughts came to a head in the early summer of 1982. Since I was learning to ask God questions and then trusting Him to answer in His time and in any manner He chose to speak to me, the question, "Should I be married and if so, WHO would you have me marry?" often swirled around in my mind. During this period of time, I had been encouraged to ask the Lord for specific direction by asking Him for a sign of some kind, a sign only He and I would be aware of. The sign I asked the Lord for regarding potential marriage? "Lord, if you want me to be married, would you speak through my parents?" Innocuous enough, yet unfathomable to me in the smallness of my faith. My belief was that this was such a huge thing to ask that I would be safe for a while!

Having offered the Lord my request, I gave it no more thought. Two weeks passed, and I had all but forgotten about it when I went home for the weekend to visit my parents. After church that Sunday, we were sitting around the table talking after lunch when the conversation suddenly drifted to the topic of marriage! My younger brother had just become engaged, so it was natural to talk about the subject. The conversation progressed along very normal lines—that is, until my mother made the statement, "We always thought you would be the first one to be married." Shocked and feeling put on the spot, I flippantly replied, "Well, who do you think I should have married?" Imagine my disbelief when my mother, without missing a beat, replied, "Your dad and I always thought Melinda was the one for you."

I don't know if anyone else could tell, but I suddenly felt flushed and light-headed as the gravity of what had just been spoken sank in. A mere two weeks earlier, had I not asked the Lord to speak to me about marriage through my parents? And had my mother really just made the statement I thought I had heard? Had God truly answered my prayer? In that moment my mind began to reel with the possibility. All I could think of was how impossible that would be since I had burned the bridge between Melinda and myself in a very hurtful and final way. Driving home, the thought kept racing through my head, though, saying, "You asked me to speak through your parents. What you heard was real. Trust Me, son."

All night long I wrestled with those words. Feeling fearful and lacking in faith due to the manner in which I had cut things off with Melinda, I felt little, if any, confidence in pursuing a relationship with her. Putting myself in her place, I told myself I would never speak to me again! Still, I couldn't stop thinking about the very specific prayer I'd prayed and the very specific way in which it had been so convincingly answered. And then I got another bright idea. "Lord, I know you answered my prayer, but I'm so reticent to even approach Melinda. Father, you spoke to me through my parents. Would you speak to me—confirm Your will—through her parents?"

I know. Oh, ye of little faith! That's exactly how I felt, too. But as I look back, I think that for where I was at that time, that was a very bold thing for me to do! Since those were the days before cell phones, all I had to go on were two very basic facts. I had heard that Melinda was living with her mom since her parents divorced, and I had her mother's address! So, I carefully penned a letter, addressing it to her mother, Sheila. In that letter, I simply stated fact. I had hurt her daughter. I knew I did not deserve her daughter. I desired to seek her forgiveness. I wanted to pursue a relationship with her daughter and had nothing but good intentions for her. I wanted her permission to contact Melinda again.

Little did I know, but Melinda had recognized my handwriting on the envelope and had called her mom at work and read it to her over the phone! The next thing I know, I received a call from Sheila giving me her whole-hearted permission to pursue her daughter. Driving down to Mesquite, Texas, I met with Melinda and her mom and sought Melinda's forgiveness. I told her I wanted to pursue a relationship with her, telling her God had done a mighty work in my heart and life and that I wanted to prove to her that she could trust me. Of course, I deftly avoided telling her the specifics of my past. Why would I do that?

My friend, Chuck, had been getting counsel for me from a trusted mentor of his. It was one of those "I have a friend who struggles with same-sex attraction, but he's afraid of others finding out his struggle so what should I tell him?" counseling sessions. His advice? Quoting Psalm 103:12 NASB, he said, "As far as the east is from the west, so far has He removed our transgressions from us." Translation? God has forgotten about your sin; so should you. Don't dredge it up anymore.

That was great news to me! I never had to tell anyone ever again! I was FREE! The only problem was that real marriage requires real intimacy, not just sexual intimacy. I was about to head into a marriage expecting utter intimacy while holding back the deepest part of my heart—a part of me that only Melinda could help me heal.

THE WEDDING NIGHT
AND TRUE INTIMACY

Melinda came to Oklahoma City to visit me in either late July or early August of 1982, and I'd already planned to step out on faith and pop the question! Since I was about to begin a new job as a fourth-grade teacher at a private Christian school, I had very little money but had talked my dad into co-signing for a loan for me so I could buy Melinda a ring. Carefully planning the evening, we went out to eat, and afterward I told her I wanted to show her a local park. Whenever we were in the car, we would sing together; it just seemed natural and appropriate, and I always had a 2nd Chapter of Acts cassette in my tape player. She didn't seem to notice my nervousness as we sang our way to the park. She didn't seem to notice that I just happened to have my guitar with me. It appeared quite normal for her that I would say, "Let's go sit in the park, and I'll play while we sing."

Making our way to a concrete picnic table, I unpacked the guitar and casually told her I had a song for her. As I began to sing the song, I couldn't stop shaking. My voice was trembling as were my hands. I'm sure she thought, "What is wrong with this guy?" But as the words stumbled out of my mouth, she was able to translate the intention of my feeble attempt at singing. Finishing the song, I knelt down and presented her the ring box and asked, "Will you marry me?"

We were married one year later on August 12, 1983. Of course, one of the most asked questions to myself was, *Will I be able to perform sexually?* That entire year became a year of intense self-discovery concerning my true masculine identity. The conclusion I kept coming back to each time the question arose in my mind was, *God set me free. God put us together. I trusted Him to do that. I will trust Him with my body, trusting Him to cause all things to work together for His good. ALL things.* That was honestly my prayer. And I trusted Him.

The night of our wedding was intensely beautiful to me on so many levels. Liberating. Exhilarating. Faith-building. What I'm about to share with you is something only Melinda and I have known for the past thirty years of our marriage, but I feel compelled by the Lord to share these things with you concerning our intimacy. Don't worry, I'll be discreet. Just suffice it to say that I was more than a bit nervous as we entered our honeymoon suite at the Anatole in Dallas. Feeling hungry and trying to quell the nerves with distraction, I ordered a hamburger and fries. For trying to ease into THE MOMENT and calm myself, the hamburger really did help.

Allowing myself to be seen naked and unashamed was a new thing for me, and seeing Melinda and her great beauty set me at ease immediately. As we settled into bed, an amazing thing began to happen for me. My body began to respond to the truth I'd been learning about myself. This simple realization—that what God called truth was indeed MY truth—filled my heart with a passion and, dare I say, a level of masculinity that I'd only dreamt of until that moment. As we caressed each other, my body began to surge with feelings of peace and utter trust, and my thoughts gave way to sheer ecstasy. As our initial love-making came to a sweet close and we cuddled, I was overcome with emotion. Melinda didn't quite understand nor could I tell her, other than to say, "For the first time in my sexual life, I feel no guilt or shame."

In my mind, my freedom was utter and complete. That night, I had eradicated the last vestiges of self-loathing concerning my past, and I fully embraced my heterosexuality! Although Melinda and I enjoyed a very healthy sex life, I saw no reason to share my past with her. In my mind, my past was done—a closed chapter of my life. Charging full-steam ahead with our lives, we both intensely enjoyed our physical relationship. Both having been through such hurtful pasts and both having felt so robbed of much of our youth—robbed of so much life—we determined early on in our marriage that we would give ourselves freely to each other. If she needed my body, it was hers; if I needed her body, hers was mine— no holding back. We took this passage of God's Word as our own in order to enhance our intimacy: "The wife does not have authority over her own body, but the husband *does;* and likewise also the husband does not have authority over his own body, but the wife *does.* Stop depriving one another, except by agreement for a time, so that you may devote yourselves to prayer, and come together again so that Satan will not tempt you because of your lack of self-control" (1 Corinthians 7:4-5 NASB).

We took it to the next level as well, telling God that we would receive all the life—children—He would give us in the process. And the babies began to come! December 1983 became a very special time for us. It's when we found out that Melinda was pregnant with our firstborn, Israel. Our level of physical intimacy was made even more precious by the depth and manner in which we were able to learn to communicate with each other. Still, I longed for her to know me more. I actually ached to tell her about my past but felt sure she would divorce me should the truth ever come out. So, as was my custom, I put it into a song—a song whose meaning she would not fully realize for five more years.

SONG OF HOPE

Verse
If you were to pass away from this life
Where would you be in eternity?
If you knew you had the choice to be totally free
Where would you be?

You shouldn't listen to fear
'Cause you're only denyin'
Your heart the peace you can't get
Yet you're dying for
Listen to love and then you stop tryin'
'Cause Jesus is dyin' to love you!
Chorus
And I wish I could take your heart into my heart
I wish I could show you just how good it feels
To let go of the things you know are killing you
And cling to the only One Who can heal
But I know if I did then it wouldn't be you
'Cause you, you're the only one choosing for you
It's true!

Verse
If you were to walk away and never hear Him again
And die in your sin
And you found you in Satan's Hell with no one to tell
You know it too well

You shouldn't listen to fear
'Cause you're only denyin'
Your heart the peace you can't get
Yet you're dying for
Listen to love and then you stop tryin'
'Cause Jesus is dyin' to love you!

Chorus
And I wish I could take your heart into my heart
I wish I could show you just how good it feels

To let go of the things you know are killing you
And cling to the only One Who can heal
But I know if I did then it wouldn't be you
'Cause you, you're the only one choosing for you
It's true!

Bridge
Listen, He's calling to the lonely
And He's the only Way, the Truth, the Life
Listen, He's crying, too
But for who? Could it be you?

Chorus
And He wants to take your heart into His heart
He wants to show you just how good it feels
To let go of the things you know are killing you
And cling to the only One Who can heal
Yes, He knows all the pain that your heart's going through
Yes, He knows and He's risen and calling for you!
It's true!
It's true!

Words & Music: Dennis Jernigan
December 6, 1983
II Peter 3:9

It was seven years and four children into our marriage before TRUE intimacy took place. During the summer of July 1988, I'd been leading worship at our church. During a time of teaching, our pastor presented us with the opportunity to deal with past issues in our lives. So, I found myself at the altar. In anguish over the fact that I felt completely free from same-sex attraction, yet not free enough to trust God with that truth as it related to others I was in relationship with, I was in tears. Before I knew it, two men I trusted were with me at the altar. Scott was on my left, and Wayne was on my right. Without telling them the specific nature of my past, I assured them it was indeed sordid and that I was convinced others would reject me should they find out, especially my wife!

Wayne simply quoted Psalm 107:1–2 to me, not knowing it was one of my favorite passages of Scripture from my days of singing through the Psalms. "Oh give thanks to the LORD, for He is good, For His lovingkindness is everlasting. Let the redeemed of the LORD say so, Whom He has redeemed from the hand of the adversary." He went on to simply say, "Dennis, if you're redeemed, what does it matter what you're redeemed from as long as you're redeemed?" All through the rest of that evening my mind was consumed with that truth. If I'm redeemed, what does it matter what I'm redeemed from?

As we made our way home and tucked the babies into bed, I sang each one of them to sleep, overwhelmed with my Father's love for me—love now being poured out from me onto my own children. Melinda could tell I was nervous as I crawled into bed. After a few tense moments, she asked me, "What is it?" And the grace of God was on me to go for it.

"Do you remember how we agreed to never talk about the specifics of our past—how we thought it would do more damage than good? I don't think that's true. I want you to know me—I mean REALLY know me. And I want to really know you. And we can't do that if we're hiding anything from each other."

She was fearful, I could tell. But I assured her I didn't want to hurt her and that I thought somehow God would make it even better between us if I could share with her the one last shred of grave clothes I still walked in concerning my past. She simply said, "Go on."

"Remember the *Song of Hope*—'How I wish I could take your heart into my heart?' Remember when we broke up in college, and I told you there were things about me—about my past—that you would be better off not knowing? Well, I can't get around God's Word. He has led me to the conclusion that if I can't say what I've been redeemed from, then I don't really trust Him. And I want to share with you because as much as I trust Him, I trust you, too."

Silence.

After a few moments, I simply said, "In my past, I struggled with homosexuality."

Silence . . . broken by the sweetest words I'd ever heard from my wife.

"Is that all?"

IS THAT ALL?!?!?! Was she kidding me!

She went on. "Now I can tell you my junk., and we can move on."

That night I discovered the greatest depth of intimacy known to man. I discovered that I could nakedly trust my God and that I could nakedly trust my wife. What had been a truly intimate and passionate marriage before now became a raging, uncontainable inferno of intimacy between two people and their God—an intimacy I'd never imagined possible in this life.

I thought I'd finally arrived until . . .

THERE IS ALWAYS MORE

Our marriage became somehow stronger after I shared my struggles with my wife, but Father had more in store for me than I had ever imagined and would use the things I'm most ashamed of to bring even greater healing to my already healing soul. After the night of honesty with Melinda, my heart was greatly encouraged. If my wife knew about my past and still loved me, then what did anything else matter? The one I needed the most was firmly with me and for me and on my side! In fact, the level of freedom it brought me just to have one other significant person know me and love me filled me with such confidence that I began to consider who else might need to know about my past.

The first person who came to mind was my pastor, Jerry. Melinda and I had met Jerry one day when he came to our house to invite us to his church, a small inner city church of about fifty people. By that time, Melinda and I were pretty much done with playing church—done with religion and performance—and craved real relationship. I simply dismissed Jerry and tried to graciously close the door on him without hurting his feelings, but he played a trump card. "I hear you like Keith Green and 2nd Chapter of Acts," he said. I let him in, and we talked for an hour about those two powerful ministries in my life.

As he left, he invited us to come and worship on Wednesday night, assuring us that we would truly love the relational worship.

The following Wednesday night, we made our way there. The group was small but very welcoming. As the time for worship came, a man got up and called the church into a time of business meeting. Melinda and I looked at each other and didn't have to say a word. We felt a sense of religion come over us and simply got up, picked up our infant son, and headed for the door. Jerry saw us leaving and made a bee-line for us. "Where are you going?" he asked with a look of disbelief. "We're done with religion—rules and regulations. We just want Jesus," was my reply. "The business meeting will last only five minutes, and then we'll worship. Trust me. You'll be glad you came."

Sitting back down, sure enough, the business meeting was short and sweet. And then the worship pastor, Paul, got up and began to lead in a short worship chorus. As the lyrics began, sweetness and a simplicity began to fill the room.

> It's beginning to rain hear the voice of the Father
> Saying whosoever will come and drink from the water
> I will pour My Spirit out on My sons and My daughters
> If you're thirsty and dry lift your hands to the sky
> It's beginning to rain
> Composed by William & Gloria Gaither/Aaron Wilburn
> ©1979 Gaither Music/First Monday Music

I could not stop crying. All I could do was thank God for this small group of people who didn't seem to care that anyone else saw them openly loving Jesus, openly and outwardly expressing their love for Him. And it was very obvious that they believed He loved them as well. We fell in love with this group of people that night and felt we finally had a home. For the next eight years, we called this group home. And since I was done performing for approval, I felt no need to be a big part of the worship team. For the first year, the most I did was an occasional solo. Mostly I was content to play my violin as a simple offering of worship to my God. God was teaching me to find my source of life in Him and not in my performance. Just BEING was truly enough for the first time in my life.

One Sunday morning, as was our practice as a worship team, we were gathered in a small room next to the sanctuary to pray. The band was there. The praise singers were there. The pastor and the worship leader were there. As we gathered in a circle to begin seeking God together, worship pastor Paul asked to share something. We all respected Paul so much, being such a servant and so loving and encouraging to everyone all the time. But his tone concerned me. He seemed to be more solemn and serious than usual.

"God has put it on my heart that I'm standing in someone else's place as worship leader. In fact, that person can't assume his rightful place as long as I'm standing in it."

His words felt so heavy to my soul. The entire room felt it at once. The looks on each face said it all. "Paul is resigning, and we're about to be devastated."

He went on. "And God has shown me who is to be standing in this place instead of me."

We were all in shock by this point, but my shock turned to disbelief with his next sentence.

"That person is Dennis Jernigan."

Like being slammed with a baseball bat to my head, I was stunned. Before I could even respond, Pastor Jerry chimed in. "God has spoken the same thing to me. And you are to begin today."

Like a deer caught in headlights, I walked zombie-like to the podium and stood and directed the songs that had already been selected for the service. Though I loved all the songs and felt them whole-heartedly, they didn't express what I felt that day. Immediately after the service, I went to pastor Jerry and said, "If this is truly God's will, then I must lead out of my giftings. Let me lead from the piano next week. In that way, I can flow from song to song as the Spirit leads." That was in 1986, and I've not gotten up from the piano since!

After that day, the Lord began to pour music into my heart specifically for our little body of people. Songs were born for grieving people. Songs were born for people trapped in addiction. Songs were born for people who had been wounded or betrayed. Songs began to be born for specific sermons. Songs were born for situations born of my own life that I couldn't openly share with anyone else until that night I shared with Melinda.

After sharing with Melinda, I began to feel a sense of urgency to tell others. Not only did my heart feel lighter by sharing the load with others, but I felt a responsibility to let those I was in ministry with know so they could take whatever steps they deemed necessary to find someone to take my place. Having already been worship pastor for almost two years to this point, I felt compelled to tell Jerry of my past, planning to step down from my leadership role.

Jerry's response? "You need to share this with the entire body." His reasoning? "Others will find grace to share their own hurts and failures if you will share yours." That night, on the thirteenth of July, 1988, I did just that. Jerry told the church that I'd be sharing something significant with them. Shakily and tensely, feeling as if I would pass out the entire time, I managed to tell my story, and it took all of ten minutes that first time. As I walked down from the podium, I expected to be shunned and had planned on resigning as soon as I could talk with Jerry. But something amazing happened.

Jerry asked me to stand up and face the people, and then he invited them to come, one by one, and share with me what my story had meant to them. Expecting to be treated with disgust and embarrassment, especially by my male friends, I was stunned into tears when my best friend, Greg, came to me and hugged me with all his might and wouldn't let me go. Healing flowed through me in that moment. And I thought I'd been healed before! But as usual, Father had more.

A common thread began to be woven through each person's words that night. Standing there after I had shared for over an hour, I listened to story after story. "Thank you for sharing. Your courage gave me the courage to seek healing for an abortion I had when I was in high school."

"Thank you for sharing. I, too, struggle with same-sex attraction, and I want out. I'm going to fight for my freedom."

"Thank you for sharing. For the first time, I feel like healing is possible. I was sexually assaulted as a teenager and never told anyone because I thought it was my fault. I felt I was too soiled to even approach God. I felt too wounded to even trust Him to touch my broken heart, but now I'm ready to let Him heal me completely."

On and on the stories went. And soon I began to hear from others who had not even been there that night! And then it dawned on me that I should probably tell my parents next because I would rather them hear it from me than from second-hand sources. So I went home to Boynton and asked my parents if I could talk with them. I remember being so afraid to talk to them that I almost blew it. Dad had already gone to bed, and I knew I wouldn't have a chance the next day, so I asked my mom to join me and Dad in their bedroom. Daddy was already under the covers, but I summoned up the courage somehow and sat on the bed next to him.

"Remember when I was having a hard time in high school and remember not knowing how to help me in my moodiness when I was in college? There was a reason for all of that."

Dying on the inside, yet knowing that of all the people I had shared with, my parents deserved to know most of all. I simply told them, "I struggled with homosexuality and didn't know how to deal with it; I didn't know how to share it with you. But I'm free now! God made a way out for me, and I wanted you to know. Thanks for standing with me even when you must've thought I was losing my mind."

I wasn't ready for what happened next. My dad—my non-emotionally expressive dad—took me by the hand and said, "Is that all?"

Mom was crying, and Daddy was choking up. Both hugged me, and we sat there for a couple of seconds taking in what had just happened. Then my mom simply said, "I love you, Dennis." And then, my dad, still holding my hand, squeezed my hand and said, "I love you, son."

That's all I needed to hear from my parents. I was in hog heaven now! Feeling as if nothing could hold me back, I determined I needed to tell my three younger brothers next, so I decided to simply write them a letter detailing all I had experienced. As I sent those letters off, I thought it might be a good idea to send a copy to James Robison, a popular minister with an influence upon millions of people. Why? James and his worship leader, Jeanne Rogers, had been using some of my music in their Bible conferences, and I thought they could quietly stop using my music so as to not bring embarrassment to their ministry.

Later the next week, I received a phone call from a friend frantically telling me to turn on the TV because James Robison was reading my letter on national television! Suddenly I had a ministry— whether I wanted it or not. Who would've thought that God would take my greatest shame and share it as a means of helping others who struggled with unwanted *anything*, and for His glory?! Only an amazing and loving God could do that!

> As for you, you meant evil against me, *but* God meant it for good in order to bring about this present result, to preserve many people alive. (Genesis 50:20 NASB)

And still there was more.

THE HEALING OF MEMORIES

There really is always more. Since my initial healing, life has become less of a burden and more of an adventure. I've learned to stop seeing life through the lens of the world—or through the lens of the Enemy of God—and to see each and every situation and circumstance through the lens of the Kingdom of God. What does that mean? I want to see life from God's perspective rather than solely from my human perspective. From a human point of view, I see a lot of hurt and failure and death and destruction, but from God's point of view, I see a lot of healing and triumph and life and restoration! I can either see what God sees and respond with hope, or I can see what the Enemy wants me to see and walk in despair.

How did I learn this? While still at the church in Oklahoma City, pastor Jerry taught us to pray using the Lord's Prayer as a pattern.

> Pray, then, in this way: "Our Father who is in heaven, Hallowed be Your name. Your kingdom come. Your will be done, On earth as it is in heaven. Give us this day our daily bread. And forgive us our debts, as we also have forgiven our debtors. And do not lead us into temptation, but

deliver us from evil. For Yours is the kingdom and the power and the glory forever. Amen. (Matthew 6:9-13 NASB).

For eight years, we gathered at 6:00 AM, Monday through Friday, to pray, and I helped lead that prayer time. As we asked the Lord to bring His Kingdom into our lives in a tangible way, we began to experience freedom and insight to successful living that I'd never experienced or seen before! During that time, it dawned on me the reality of the words of Jesus in Matthew 6:33 NASB, that says, "But seek first His kingdom and His righteousness, and all these things will be added to you." To seek to know the Kingdom, I reasoned, I had better be seeking to know the King of that Kingdom, Jesus Christ! So my journey became even more intimate and even more liberating. Overcoming same-sex attraction became such a small portion of my life because I began to discover that the true needs of my life were more basic than the sexual temptations I experienced, and that even those fleeting temptations would wane if I met my needs through Jesus.

As the years went on and I deepened my walk with God, the freedom I experienced went to places I'd only dreamed of. It was as if what I'd experienced on the night of November 7, 1981, was merely the beginning of my liberation! That night the doors were blown off of my personal hell and prison. What transpired in the years to come has been nothing less than Father tearing down the prison walls in ways I did not even know I needed.

Even though I'd been walking in freedom since 1981, the extent of that freedom was yet to dawn on me. Between 1989 and 1990, I was telling my story more and more in public forums. With each sharing, I felt a bit more free than the previous time. It was amazing to experience, yet I still had moments of despair and depression and anxiety. This was bewildering to me because I had considered myself free. If I was so free, why did I still battle such things? After all, I knew who I was in Christ, and I knew Whose I was as His child!

By this time, I'd become fully aware that my battleground was not my physical body, but rather my *mind*. For this reason, I'd come to trust the Lord in faith even when my feelings didn't match up with what I knew to be truth. As I sought the Lord about this one day, I heard Him say, "Son, what are you thinking about when despairing, depressing, anxious thoughts come?"

That was an easy one to answer. "Lord, why did you allow homosexuality in my life? Where were you when I was five years old and that man exposed himself to me? You say in Your Word that you will never leave me and never forsake me, but it seems like you did. And how about when my grandmother died? You left me utterly alone. And why did my dad never tell me he loved me until after I was married? And that incident with my college mentor—where were you in that?"

Every depressing and despairing anxious thought was attached to a memory of wounding in my past. "What do I do with these thoughts, Father?"

"You give them to Me, son. Make a list of all the times you feel I've forsaken or forgotten you, and I'll show you my point of view when the time is right. Just make your list and trust Me."

So I did. That list became several pages long. Single line memories. Single moments of hurt. Moments of betrayal. Moments of humiliation. Moments of shame. Moments I'd carried since childhood. After my list was complete, I felt exhausted yet one step closer to God in honest intimacy. Lighter, freer, yet still lost in a fog of wondering how and when God would reveal His truth to me. After I made my list and felt I'd gotten everything out in the open, I gave the list to Father and asked Him to show me His point of view whenever He would. I didn't have to wait long.

Two weeks passed, and I honestly hadn't thought much about the list. Just making it had taken away some of the feelings I'd been dealing with. In addition, I'd been invited to come to Boynton,

Oklahoma, my hometown, to lead a community-wide night of praise. Full of anticipation at getting to share my music with the people I'd grown up with, yet slightly apprehensive in knowing full well I might have to see face to face some of the people who had hurt me in the past, I prepared for the night.

I should've known that once I got there things would be fine, but once again I allowed the subtle lies of the Enemy to invade my mind. As I'd learned by that time, I battled through the lies with the truth and faced the giants of fear and shame and past hurts with grace and favor of the Lord. The night went so well. With only about fifty people in attendance and knowing most of the people personally, the night was at once intimate and healing for me. Soaking in the triumph of having faced those giants, I was very refreshed after the concert of worship. But God had more refreshing for me than I'd bargained for.

After the concert, a little gray-haired lady, June Smith, approached me and said, "Isn't it wonderful how your grandmother Jernigan's prayers have been answered?"

Somewhat dumbfounded, I asked her what she was talking about.

She said, "You don't know?"

"Don't know what?" I replied.

"Remember when you were a little boy and would go to your grandmother's house and play the piano?"

"Yes," I said. "Those are some of my most precious memories."

Going on, she asked, "And did you know she would stand behind you and pray for you?"

"How do you know that?" was all I could say.

"Every week for years, son, she would come to our weekly women's prayer meetings at church and tell us how she would ask the Lord to use you in the area of worship and music for His kingdom and for His glory, and she would ask us to agree with her in prayer. And, Dennis, we still do!" As of this writing, two of those little ladies are still alive and continue to pray for me, and I'm fifty-four years old! Grandma died when I was thirteen!

Instantly, all I could think of was the list I'd made just two weeks earlier and how I'd asked God to show me where He had been when my grandmother died—why He had abandoned me in that way. Suddenly my mind was flooded with truth as I heard Father say, "Son, I've had you covered in prayer since day one. I multiplied your grandmother's prayers. I NEVER forsook you, not even for a moment."

Each memory that I'd placed on that list began to come into what I call a Kingdom perspective. When I was five, someone had protected me from that man's touch. All the teasing and humiliation I went through in high school had not been in vain. I began to see those things as opportunities for growth rather than for being beaten down. The shame I'd felt due to my willful disobedience of God was suddenly washed away by the truth of God's love for me. Even the wounding at the hand of my college mentor came into a different light as I allowed Father to show me how He could take even my greatest pain and sorrow and bring from it my greatest healing and joy. And then it hit me: I would never understand nor appreciate the sweetness of the rain had I never gone through the desert episodes of my life. But still He was not through.

As Father would have it, He began to nudge me into talking with my dad about things that had happened when I was a boy, like why he couldn't talk with me about sex. And the "biggie"—why he could never verbally tell me he loved me. Because I was traveling more and more by this time, sharing my story and my music, I had the opportunity to take my dad on one of these ministry trips. Having him all to myself in my truck, I asked the Lord for grace, and then I asked Daddy all the questions I'd been so afraid to ask him when I was younger.

"Daddy, why did you never tell me you loved me when I was growing up?" I asked, my voice shaking and my heart thumping, afraid of what he might say. But I had to know.

"Well, my dad never told me, so I didn't know *how* to tell you."

With one simple honest question and one simple honest answer, my dad and I healed a generational wound in our family. My dad now has no trouble telling me how he feels about me. A man of few words to this day, all I needed to hear were those three little words. I would've been forever happy to have heard them only one time, having lived a lifetime without them to that point!

Another thing God began to do? He had me to forgive those who had hurt me. I found that easier to do when I realized that NOT forgiving them was not punishing them one iota, but it was keeping ME locked away in the prison of my own mind! I was the only one being punished! What freedom I found in simply releasing those who had hurt me.

Yet Father still was not through. He simply said, "There's one more person you need to forgive, son."

"Who is that, Father?" I asked.

"Yourself," was all He said.

Part of my feelings of despair and depression had stemmed not only from past hurts but from how I still held myself responsible for my past choices. And indeed I am responsible for my choices, but I had continued punishing myself from time to time not realizing I had received God's forgiveness but had not forgiven myself! In a sense, MY standards were somehow higher than God's! What a liberation day it was when I simply forgave myself and moved on.

I discovered that day that there is only one time and one thing for which a believer should give up all hope. You want to know when and what that is? A believer should give up the hope of EVER changing his past; it cannot be done. I discovered I'd been wasting far too much of my time consumed with the what-ifs rather than moving on into the journey God calls this life! I am not alone—never have been; never will be. He has been with me every step of the way on this incredible journey, and I feel as if I'm just beginning.

I am who my Father says I am. My past does not define me. The gay community does not define me. The government does not define me. My feelings do not define me. My circumstances do not define me. People do not define me. Even I do not define me. Only One has that honor, and He calls me His own.

I've been utterly, irrevocably changed—signed, sealed, delivered—a child of the King who has decided to stop sitting beneath the table of life and settling for the crumbs that fall beneath. I am a child of the King of Kings, and my Father has set a table before me—in THIS life—in the presence of even my enemies, and He welcomes me to sit and dine fully with Him. Anytime. Anywhere. Under any circumstances. I am His. This is my life, and it speaks for itself.

WHAT I BELIEVE ABOUT SAME-SEX ATTRACTION

This is my point of view, and the last time I checked, I still have the freedom to express myself. If you don't agree with me, that's fine; I respect your right to not agree. But don't belittle me because of that disagreement; I would never do that to you. I find it incredulous that the gay community that calls for tolerance and compassion for their point of view is the least tolerant and compassionate toward any view that's different than their own.

The bottom line for me was that I simply didn't want to be gay, and when I realized that I'd been duped by the Liar into believing something about myself that Father God never intended, I began the most incredible journey anyone could imagine. And I wouldn't trade what I've found for ANYTHING. The Enemy of God, the Liar, tried to rob me of the deepest human intimacy I've ever known, the intimacy between a man and a woman. The intimacy I experienced in the homosexual life was never as satisfying—never. And I believe that's because for me the gay life was a counterfeit, something less than God's best.

As I've endeavored to put into writing my life story, I've become overwhelmed with all God has given me concerning life and liberty and love and joy. Thinking about all that I've endured to get here, I can honestly say that it's been worth it. Knowing Jesus Christ intimately has been worth every struggle and sorrow and torment of soul that I've been through. Think about what the Liar tried to rob me of—my wife, my nine children, my joy.

My belief that freedom is possible stems not only from my personal experience but also, and perhaps more so, from a worldview not based on human wisdom. My understanding of my sexuality is not dependent upon my past experiences or present circumstances, nor is it defined by anything that might tempt me for a fleeting moment. My understanding of my one-time dependence upon same-sex attraction is that it was born of true and honest needs for male intimacy and affirmation being met in unnatural ways. Every boy needs to learn how to be a man and learns it best from an older male. When my perception of masculinity became skewed by wrong perceptions at an early age, I came to believe I was different from other boys and, therefore, different in every way. The need for male affirmation became sexualized, and sexual stimulation became the go-to remedy for meeting those needs. Instant gratification supersedes self-control when one's foundation is anything other than a God-centric foundation or point of view. Man becomes the highest. Man becomes the focus. Self becomes the ultimate. Yet that was never the way Father God intended for those needs to be met.

After my initial freedom, and to help myself understand my true masculinity, I began to hang around with masculine men. I studied the real thing rather than the counterfeit. What I discovered was that every man, regardless of his perceived sexual orientation, has a need to connect with another masculine soul. Boys learn to be men by being with men who know how to guide them to manhood. In nature we see it vividly portrayed in the elephant world. When a male elephant is born, he lives with his mother in the herd of mostly females until he reaches a certain age, around two years old. At that time, his mother drives him from the herd and toward an all-male herd comprised of older, mature males. In this manner, he learns how to be a male elephant. If for some reason that young male doesn't attach to an older, wiser male group, he'll not learn how to control his masculinity and will become rogue. It's the rogue elephant that tends to run amok because he has no one to show him how to harness his true elephant masculinity. I was rogue for far too long because I was utterly self-focused and lacked ultimate self-control.

When I discovered who I was, when I began to think as Father intended me to think, the old ways began to fall away from me, and I began to experience true and realistic masculinity. In nature we see a mighty oak and think about all the time and growth it required to get to the massive expanse it enjoys, but we must remember that everything that would become the oak was already IN the acorn. The acorn just needed time and the proper conditions in which to grow to become the mighty oak. So it was with me. When I was born again in faith on November 7, 1981, I was in essence like that tiny acorn. Everything I would become was already planted in me; I just needed time and proper conditions in which to grow into who God intended me to be all along.

Logically, I look at the body of a man and the body of a woman and see how they were created to fit and work together. The body of a man was never intended to fit with the body of another man, nor was the body of a woman intended to mesh with that of another woman. In reality, the act of sex was intended for procreation, pure and simple. Anything else is a perversion of the use God intended. In reality, a man having sex with another man or a woman having sex with another woman actually cancels out life rather than creates life.

When I was a boy and I was labeled as effeminate, the things I perceived that made me appear as feminine in nature were actually things like emotional sensitivity, artistic gifts and talents, and my ability to empathize with the feelings of others. All of those things were gifts from God intended for use in God's kingdom and for the good of others. I allowed the Enemy to get me to use those gifts in ways and for purposes God never intended—perversion. All perversion is, is using the things God intended for holy purposes in unholy manners. Sex was intended to be a good thing. Emotions were intended to be good things. My entire being and make-up was intended for good purposes. I simply settled into the wrong usage of those things by trying to meet my own needs in ways those needs were never intended to be met.

I've also determined that what the world calls love and what God calls love are usually two very different things. In the eyes and minds of the world, the greatest expression of love is the sexual act between any two consenting parties. In God's eyes and mind, the greatest expression of love is the laying down of life, and the sexual act of love is reserved for the marriage bed—between one man and one woman. I know, I know, the divorce rate is as high in the church as in the world, but just because God's people seem to fail so miserably at times does not negate the Lord's desire for our best in the area of marriage and sex.

It has been in the writing of my life story that I've become even MORE convinced of what I believe. The misconception is that I hate those who disagree with me; nothing could be further from the truth! As proudly as the gay community applauds those who "come out" and embrace homosexuality openly, I proudly applaud those who "come out" of a formerly homosexual identity in search of freedom from it. How is my applause any less plausible than that of the gay community? It angers me to no end to think that there are so many in the gay community who want me to fail, to fall back into homosexuality, rather than to rejoice with me in my desire for freedom and for the freedom I've found. It seems hypocritical to me. Just sayin'.

Still, I have detractors say to me, "What if you're wrong? If you're wrong, aren't you doing more damage than good?" To them I say what if YOU are wrong? What if you're actually keeping countless people from freedom from something they don't actually desire to be? I've met hundreds of men and women through the years who, like me, don't want to be gay. What about their right to pursue a different life for themselves? Since I'm being honest, it was

WHAT I BELIEVE ABOUT SAME-SEX ATTRACTION

actually pressure from some of my gay friends who seemed to despise me for wanting out who caused me to have suicidal thoughts. Shouldn't a person have the right to choose whom they will follow, whom they will serve, and who they will be?

I've had people say to me, "You were never truly gay. You made up the story to sell music." Really? If I were going to make up a story, it certainly would be better and much more glamorous than the one you've just read. To sell music? Are you kidding me? Think about that in relation to the secular world. How much of the pop music of today caters exclusively to the gay community? The music of one who came out of homosexuality is not that popular in Christian circles. Remember, this topic is one the church would rather someone else deal with!

I've been told, "You are bisexual. You're just giving sway to your masculine side now." To them I simply say that I was never attracted to females at all until God began to deal with my self-perception and to show me my true and intended identity.

On several occasions I've heard this: "You've been brainwashed." And to those individuals I have to say that I agree! I've had my mind cleansed of the old ways of thinking and have put on the way of thinking God intended all along.

"You're still tempted, therefore you're still gay." To that I say this: homosexuality is a temptation, NOT an identity! While I can't forget the things I've already experienced in my former life of homosexuality, I've come to understand that temptation was never meant to define me. I now find homosexual temptation minuscule. Let's face it, where can I turn today where I'm NOT confronted with same-sex attraction? But it lost its power over me a long time ago. If temptation comes, I know Father has something great for me that the Enemy is trying to rob me of. In that moment, temptation becomes a catalyst to intimacy with God. Sin avoided. Who I am boils over into my entire being. Enemy defeated. Enough said. Jesus was tempted in every manner yet without sin. Temptation defines no one. Ultimately, temptation reveals a very real need, but I've learned

185

to meet those needs in the manner God intended. I can honestly say that it's difficult for me to believe I was ever gay. Again, just sayin'.

One more thing. Have you ever wondered why there's so much homosexuality within the creative arts? I have. And I have a couple of thoughts on that. Since I operate from a God-centric point of reference, I believe God has an Enemy, Satan, who is the deceiver of mankind. If I were the Enemy, and I wanted to get my message out to the most people, the message that man is the utmost and highest, then I would go after the most creative people I could find! Couple that with the proven reality that creative people often have the ability to think both feminine and masculine thoughts—an ability I believe was given of God not for sexual purposes but to foster deeper and more intimate, healthy relationships between individuals. Just my thoughts.

You don't have to agree with anything I've said. I'm not holding a gun to your head saying you must believe what I believe. You always have a choice. Always. We're people of choice, and I choose to love even those who hate me. I will love you regardless of where you fall on the issue of same-sex attraction. Just don't condemn me because I don't believe as you do.

I didn't want to be gay, and I discovered that I did have a choice as to Who I would allow to define me. My greatest need was for intimacy. God met that need, rendering homosexuality powerless in my life. And He continues to meet that need today. My story? This has only been the tip of the iceberg of who I am and who God is calling me to be. Stay tuned. There's always more.

THE PURPOSE OF SCARS AND WHO FATHER SAYS I AM

"Scars remind us of where we've been. They don't have to dictate where we're going."

Criminal Minds episode, September 3, 2010

"God will not look you over for medals, degrees or diplomas, but for scars."

Elbert Hubbard

"Out of suffering have emerged the strongest souls; the most massive characters are seared with scars."

Kahlil Gibran

"Every winner has scars."

Robert N. C. Nix

"It's a shallow life that doesn't give a person a few scars."

Garrison Keillor

I won't belabor the point. I've endured many wounds in life. Since we are people of choice, we always have a choice as to how we will respond to those wounds. Sometimes the pain renders us incapable of anything but self-preservation, but at some point, we'll have to choose to either allow the scar to dictate our lives or to allow the Lord to use that scar for our good and His glory. A scar that has healed completely doesn't negate what we went through. My scars? I own them. Each one represents something terrible or amazing I went through, and they're points of reference I can refer to as often as necessary that say yes, I went through that, but look what God has done.

In no way do I mean to communicate that I've arrived or that I'm as healed as I want or need to be, but I'm on my way. Apart from the grace of God, I know I'd still be in bondage. Apart from His grace, I'd fall away in a second! But it's in knowing how much He loves me that I'm compelled to keep walking the path of righteousness. If I fall, HE STILL LOVES ME right where I am. It's that kind of love that makes me want to not make the same foolish mistakes over and over again. It's in the intimacy of my relationship of faith with and through Jesus Christ that I no longer identify myself as anything less than who He says I am. To consider myself a recovering homosexual would be to tell Father He's not quite the Healer He says He is.

Who He is, is in my spiritual DNA since I'm His child by faith. A joint-heir with Christ, my Brother, my Savior, I am welcome at the table of the King, having been given the keys to an abundant life on this earth regardless of my circumstances. Quite simply, I determine to call myself—to simply BE—who Father says I am.

He is God, and we are not. We must discover Who He says He is. In the process, we discover who we are. There is no formula, no magic potion, and no quick six-step method to freedom; it is born of faith in Christ and forged in the fire of intimate relationship with Jesus Christ. In fact, there's nothing you and I can do to perform our way to freedom; it's quite simply a gift of God, born of faith and relationship. I no longer perform in order to receive His love and acceptance; I now perform because I HAVE His love and acceptance! I am who Father says I am. And exactly who do I think I am?

> I am not a sinner saved by grace. The sinner is dead; a saint has risen in his place.
>
> I am a new creation.
>
> I am healed, healing, and being healed.
>
> I consider myself free of homosexuality, even though the scars remain. Scars simply signify that a healing has taken place.
>
> I consider myself heterosexual in every sense of the word.
>
> I am NOT a recovering homosexual.
>
> I am dead to sin.
>
> I am born again.
>
> I am cleansed by the blood of Christ.
>
> I am a victor—no longer a victim.
>
> I am a runner of a race who runs to win.
>
> I am a child of destiny and purpose.
>
> I am eternally His.
>
> I am found.
>
> I am free.
>
> I am holy and righteous because He is holy and righteous.
>
> I am an overcomer.
>
> I am redeemed.
>
> I am restored.
>
> I am resurrected to new life.
>
> I am a servant of the Most High God.
>
> I am a mighty warrior.
>
> I am royalty.
>
> I am a receiver of visions and dreams.
>
> I am chosen.

I am a trophy of God's grace.

I am a delight to my God.

I am accepted.

I am a part of the Bride of Christ.

I am a kingdom seeker.

I am a singer who hears his Father singing over him.

The eternal, self-existent God
The God Who is Three in One
He who dwells in the center of your
Being is a powerful and valiant Warrior.
He has come to set you free, to keep
You safe and bring you victory.
He is cheered and He beams with
Exceeding joy and takes pleasure in your presence.
He has engraved a place for Himself in you
And there He quietly rests
In His love and affection for you.
He cannot contain Himself at the thought of you
And with the greatest of joy spins around wildly in
Anticipation over you, and has placed you above
All other creations and in the highest place of
His priorities.
In fact, He shouts and sings in
Triumph, joyfully proclaiming the gladness
Of His heart in a song of rejoicing…

ALL BECAUSE OF YOU!

Zephaniah 3:17

(Translation by Dennis Jernigan)

Dennis Jernigan is available for speaking engagements, conferences, seminars, ministry, and the sharing of his music. His ministry coordinator may be contacted at booking@dennisjernigan.com or by calling 1-800-877-0406.

Dennis has been recording his music since the late 1980s. Many of his songs are sung daily somewhere around the world. Songs like "You Are My All In All, Who Can Satisfy My Soul (There Is a Fountain)," and "We Will Worship the Lamb of Glory," to name a few. Most of his catalog is available on iTunes or at www.dennisjernigan.com.

Other books and music by Dennis Jernigan are available at www.dennisjernigan.com.

Check out these additional
titles by Innovo Publishing.

Order online at
www.innovopublishing.com.

Dealing with the S-Words by Jason Creech. Rich or poor, popular or unnoticed, we're all looking for the same thing—new life. But if young people don't get things right on the inside, they will never be the happy, successful people they were created to be. Happiness and success are an inside job. This is a book about "S-Words"—the "don't go there" words—those topics that get Sunday school teachers replaced and youth pastors fired: self-esteem, significance, sex, secrets, and suicide. Dive deeply into the topics we've all wrestled with and discover what God says about life's toughest issues.

new.u by Jason Creech. Are you just getting started as a new Christian? Then you probably have a lot of questions. In this five-week devotional, you'll discover a boat-load of answers. Learn the simplicity of the Christian life. Welcome to freedom. Welcome to the new u.

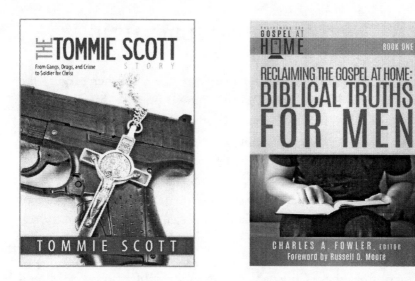

The Tommie Scott Story by Tommie Scott is the true story of a gangbanger and drug dealer nicknamed "Hit man" who worked his way through the juvenile reform system and into a California state prison by age twenty. It's the story of an angry young criminal with no remorse and no hope. And it's here--in the depths of hopeless darkness--that this story begins again with a spiritual rebirth into God's family through Jesus Christ. And the story continues today with a repentant and joyful servant, a dedicated soldier for Christ

Reclaiming the Gospel at Home: Biblical Truths for Men by Charles A. Fowler, Editor. King David's imprint on the history of Israel is significant. Scripture reveals that he was a "man after God's own heart." We see David as a young shepherd boy, a friend of Jonathan, and a servant to King Saul. Ultimately, we follow his journey as King of Israel. Many of the episodes from his life are set within the context of his often complicated family, affording opportunities to see David's personal successes as well as his heartbreaking failures. The scriptural account of his life provides many insights and reveals that biblical manhood is a noble pursuit achievable even in the most challenging of situations.

ABOUT INNOVO PUBLISHING

Innovo Publishing is a full-service Christian publisher serving the Christian and wholesome markets. Innovo creates, distributes, and markets quality hardback and paperback books, eBooks (Kindle, Nook, iPhone, iPad, ePub), audiobooks, music (CDs and MP3s), and film through traditional publishing, cooperative publishing, and independent publishing models. Innovo provides distribution, marketing, and automated order fulfillment through a network of thousands of physical and online wholesalers, retailers, bookstores, music stores, schools, and libraries worldwide including Amazon, Audible, iTunes, Rhapsody, Barnes & Noble, and many more. Innovo publishes Christian fiction and non-fiction books and wholesome books for all publishing genres. Visit Innovo at www.innovopublishing.com.

FOR A HIGHER PURPOSE

CPSIA information can be obtained at www.ICGtesting.com
Printed in the USA
LVOW08s2339200214

374557LV00005B/8/P